T0096576

# AGAINST
# THE ELEMENTS

# AGAINST THE ELEMENTS

## THE ERUPTION OF ICELANDIC FOOTBALL

### MATT McGINN

First published by Pitch Publishing, 2020

Pitch Publishing
A2 Yeoman Gate
Yeoman Way
Worthing
Sussex
BN13 3QZ
www.pitchpublishing.co.uk
info@pitchpublishing.co.uk

© 2020, Matt McGinn

Every effort has been made to trace the copyright.
Any oversight will be rectified in future editions at the
earliest opportunity by the publisher.

All rights reserved. No part of this book may be reproduced, sold
or utilised in any form or transmitted in any form or by any means,
electronic or mechanical, including photocopying, recording or
by any information storage and retrieval system, without prior
permission in writing from the Publisher.

A CIP catalogue record is available for this book
from the British Library.

ISBN 978 1 78531 720 0

Typesetting and origination by Pitch Publishing
Printed and bound in India by Replika Press Pvt. Ltd

# Contents

In memory of
Mary Hilton-Jones

# Acknowledgements

THIS BOOK would still be a harebrained idea were it not for the collaboration and support of dozens of people.

From the moment we first discussed this project in a Madrid bar, I have been hugely grateful to Joseph Fox for his travel companionship and wonderful photography. Iceland often has to be seen to be believed. Joseph's photographs capture the people, places and moments that writers far better than me would struggle to convey with words.

Jane Camillin at Pitch Publishing showed faith in the book at an uncertain time, and I thank Duncan Olner and Pete Gentry for their design and editorial input. From deCoubertin, James Corbett, Jack Gordon Brown, and Megan Pollard worked on the manuscript with imagination and skill. The guidance of Charlotte Atyeo was valuable throughout.

Thank you to everyone who gave up their time to be interviewed. Though not all feature in the final edit, each one shaped my ideas and taught me something new. For their various contributions, I am particularly grateful to: Anna Lea Friðriksdóttir, Haffi Már Sigurðsson, Ómar Smárason, Jóhann Ólafur Sigurðsson, Gregg Broughton,

Tom Dent, David Nelson and the guys at *AS English*, Svein Graff, Ólafur Garðarsson, Sandra Valsdóttir, Hulda Birna Baldursdóttir, Lúðvík Gunnarsson, Viðar Halldórsson, Birkir Már Sævarsson, Biggi Sverrisson and his crew, Lizzie Frost, Will Watt, and Darren Bentley.

Thanks most of all to my parents, Diana and Ambrose, for always encouraging me to pursue my interests and instincts, and to Alice for her kindness, support and remarkable tolerance of football.

# Introduction

THE REALITY of football often outdoes its fiction. Rarely has this been clearer than when Iceland played Albania in Reykjavík in 1990.

It was a qualifier for the 1992 European Championship. The 40-year rule of Albanian dictator Enver Hoxha had ended in 1985. Though the first free elections would not be held until March 1991, the country was beginning to establish links with the outside world. Yet the Albanian government would have been disappointed if it had hoped the football team would perform the role of a travelling embassy.

The party of 37 Albanians – made up of the senior and under-21 players – travelled to Iceland via Rome and London. The three-hour stopover at Heathrow Airport was eventful.

'By the time they got to the gate, there were watches everywhere,' one airport official said. 'They were sent on their way quickly,' a perturbed British newspaper added, 'a little wiser to the ways of a world light years from their own.'

The Albanian players had tried to board the connecting flight to Iceland with £2,000 of shoplifted duty-free goods.

They understood only the second word on the 'duty-free' signs and scooped up perfume and confectionary in the mistaken belief that it was complimentary. At least, that was the story they told police at Scotland Yard. The Albanians spent 24 hours as guests of the British Constabulary. After a fruitless search for a translator, police escorted them aboard a flight to Iceland. They still had duty-free items from Rome Airport in their possession.

The ordeal was not over. The Icelandic authorities took a dim view of the Albanian ignorance plea. The visitors' luggage was subjected to an extensive customs search and they were effectively placed under house arrest until the match, which was almost forgotten amid the furore.

It took place at Laugardalsvöllur, the national stadium, on a Wednesday evening in May. The sun was still high when the teams lined up to face the main stand for the national anthems. Short shorts and baggy jackets were the order of the day.

Now, finally, they could concentrate on the football. Or so they thought. The brass band had barely navigated one bar when a stark-naked man leapt over the barrier and ran towards the bemused away team. He performed a sort of jig in front of a captive Albanian audience. They stifled laughter as a red-faced policeman wrestled the slippery imposter to the ground. The brass band lowered their instruments. If only they had the sheet music to the Benny Hill theme.

Einar Már Guðmundsson – an Icelandic novelist – delighted in this inconceivable series of events. He imagined an Albanian writer, one or two years before the match, describing the events that transpired. He would have been ridiculed. He would have shattered the rules of Soviet realism.

'Reality is always catching realism by surprise,' Einar Már concluded. 'Reality often outdoes fiction.'

This seems an appropriate sentiment with which to introduce a book about the remarkable rise of Icelandic football.

For almost six decades the Iceland team failed to qualify for a major tournament. They bumbled along in the lower echelons of the world rankings. A win against the Faroe Islands here, a draw against Norway there. Iceland were not quite in the minnow category alongside Andorra, San Marino and the other nations for whom avoiding a drubbing means victory. But nor were they competitive.

Things began to change at the start of the 21st century. Like when a kaleidoscope is twisted, the various shapes and colours came together to form a coherent image. In 2016 the men's national team reached the quarter-final of the European Championship, beating England along the way. Two years later Iceland became the smallest nation to qualify for a World Cup. The women's team, meanwhile, have reached three consecutive European Championships and made the quarter-final in the 2013 edition.

It is worth getting demographic comparisons out of the way early. Though it would be remiss to ignore them, they have been repeated with such enthusiasm in the last five years that they have lost their impact. Iceland has a population of just over 350,000. That is roughly equivalent to Bradford or Leicester. Or, for the American reader, significantly fewer souls than live in Wyoming.

Within that context it is little wonder that Iceland has been venerated as an example of what good husbandry and governance can achieve in international football. The indoor football halls, the vast hangars that mushroom from the ground, are particularly symbolic of an innovative pragmatism. So too are the swathes of highly qualified Icelandic coaches. Icelandic soil should not be fertile for anything, let alone football.

Success on the pitch coincided with prominence off it. Iceland has grown in the collective global consciousness. The 2008 financial crisis exposed Reykjavík as a nest for a virulent strain of bacchanalian banking. Two years later the eruption of the Eyjafjallajökull volcano bellowed a cloud of ash over northern Europe. Air travel was heavily disrupted. The Kenyan economy suffered a blip because local horticulturalists could not export flowers to Europe. The FC Barcelona players travelled by bus to Milan for their Champions League semi-final against Internazionale.

Yet it seems that mild inconvenience inspires curiosity. The number of foreign visitors to Iceland almost quadrupled between 2010 and 2017 – from 488,600 to 2,224,600.

Back in 1990, such success and notoriety seemed implausible. Reality has caught Iceland by surprise beyond football.

The story continues to unravel. It is too soon to write a narrative account of the ascent of Icelandic football because the narrative is not yet over. Many of the players who were instrumental in 2016 and 2018 still play for Iceland. While the dust settles it makes sense to review the achievement thematically.

There is little to gain in ascribing value to each factor and it would be futile to establish a hierarchy of importance. History is not linear. They are all interwoven threads of the same beguiling tapestry, and the tapestry would not be complete were any one of those threads removed.

This is a book about football that strays from music to weightlifting; from a trawler called *Vestmannaey* to a volcanic eruption in 1973. There is value in the digression to other parts of Icelandic culture, history and society. It creates a lens through which we can view football. The sport becomes a richer subject – and one that makes more sense – when we take a step back from the white lines of the pitch.

## Chapter One
# Iceland v Argentina

IT IS the early hours of the morning in Kópavogur. Once a town in its own right, it is now a dangling suburb of Reykjavík. Iceland will make their World Cup debut against Argentina in 12 hours.

I sit, well fed, in Haffi and Anna's catalogue-cool apartment. The empty cocktail glasses on the table reveal the stage of the evening. The residue from espresso martini turns from brown to bronze in the lingering light. Leftovers from dinner are wrapped in foil in the fridge – pork, lamb and Icelandic horse. Haffi cooked them on the barbecue round the back. Every home has a barbecue. Icelanders seem to light them as soon as the temperature rises to double figures and the rain holds off for long enough for the charcoal to glow. Across the room, a record spins on the turntable. Is it Tame Impala, or was that the last one?

I met Haffi and Anna two days ago. We were at a match between Breiðablik and Fylkir in the *Úrvalsdeild karla*, the top division in Iceland. Haffi asked in Icelandic if he could leave his coat on the seat next to mine. I stared blankly for three seconds, feeling pangs of inadequacy, before he switched to English with a trace of Glaswegian. He studied in Glasgow in the late 2000s. A sound engineering course. Anna moved to Glasgow too. She left without the sharp accent, but with a fondness for gently mocking the 'posh' folk of Edinburgh.

Haffi and Anna embraced Glaswegian pub culture. Partly to integrate, partly to stay warm. The *kreppa* – the Icelandic word for the 2008 financial crash – had struck at home. They could not access their student loans. If they were in the pub, they could be more frugal with the heating in their flat. When he was on his own, Haffi developed a tactic to get in with the locals. If he saw two people chatting over whisky at the other end of the bar, he would ask the barman what they were drinking and order three more of the same. The barman would slide two glasses to the unsuspecting recipients. They would look along the bar to see Haffi, a glass raised in his hand. Conversation always flowed.

'It's the calm before the storm,' Anna says, as Haffi pours whisky that smells coarse and leathery, like a new equestrian saddle.

'Weather-wise?' someone responds.

'Everything-wise.'

They will go to Anna's brother-in-law's house to watch Iceland play Argentina. Haffi has already warned the family that the football will kidnap his emotions. I saw how animated he became during Breiðablik's routine 2-0 victory the evening we met. I fear for his blood pressure.

He stews in his own thoughts, stroking the strands of a wispy beard. 'This is the biggest thing ever in Icelandic sport history.' He reconsiders. 'No, just history. Ever.'

Football has already kidnapped his emotions. He is not the only one.

There was no sunrise on the morning of Iceland's World Cup debut. Daylight never faded beyond dusk. The colours on the horizon ran from yellow, through orange to a deep red, and back again.

One by one, tourists step off the coach and shiver. The glow of the previous night has reverted to grey. The stalagmite spire of Hallgrímskirkja – the brutalist church that dominates the Reykjavík skyline – blends with the cloud. A flag on the coach reveals the visitors are from Japan. They wait for their guide. Rain falls. It is a silky drizzle, finer than the bloated drops that Icelanders call 'foreign rain'.

The guide leads his mobile audience to the front of the church and the towering statue of Leif Erikson. According to the Icelandic Sagas, Erikson was the first European to discover North America, beating Christopher Columbus across the Atlantic after wind blew him east of Greenland. Now he poses for photographs, his left foot forward and chest puffed out, an axe in one hand and a sword hanging from his belt.

I leave the church behind me and wander idly down the slope towards the centre of the town. I came into the city early for two reasons. First, to test my stubborn hangover against the Atlantic breeze. Second, to feel the atmosphere of anticipation, to feel the clamour build. But everyone is somewhere else. I should have known that Icelanders are not prone to venture outside in wet weather unless there is good reason. Their ancestors spent centuries braving the elements by necessity.

Iceland v Argentina is not the first match of the day. France face Australia in the early kick-off. It has just started. I watch for a moment through the latticed window of a royal blue house. Like many houses in the old town, it looks like it has been plucked from a Monopoly board, inflated, and wrapped in corrugated iron. I squint at the score. 0-0.

This match, coupled with the drizzle, is why there are no Icelanders on the streets. There is football to watch. During the 2010 World Cup, a larger share of Icelanders watched the football than the inhabitants of any other European country. Germany and the Netherlands, two footballing thoroughbreds, completed the podium. Iceland did not even have a horse in the race, yet still outwatched the rest.

A chain mail-clad busker occupies his usual spot on the corner of Laugavegur, the commercial artery that runs through the capital. Cafes, restaurants and souvenir shops await customers. They have acknowledged the World Cup by swapping puffin tat for football tat in window displays. I turn left towards a cluster of English, Irish and American bars. Cardboard cut-outs of Harry Kane and Cristiano Ronaldo keep Uncle Sam company in the tinted window of a bar that promises the best chicken wings in town.

A poncho-clad American couple walk in the opposite direction, sucked along by the words in their guidebook. The woman recites: 'A perfect metaphor for how everyday life in Iceland ...' She walks out of earshot. I allow myself the luxury of snobbery. I am different to them, I tell myself. I am barely a tourist at all. I walk with hands-in-pockets purpose. I can hold a conversation about the absence of a natural successor to Birkir Már Sævarsson in the Iceland team.

France v Australia is on the giant screen in the old square. It has drawn an audience of six empty picnic benches. Teenage skateboarders and leatherback bikers usually congregate in the square. It is a curious coexistence. The skaters are perpetually on the brink of completing the trick they have been attempting for hours. The bikers park their Harleys in a row and study their reflections in the unblemished chrome. Even the skaters and the bikers stay at home today.

I feel vaguely disappointed at the lack of pre-match frenzy, but suspect that it peaked several hours earlier in downtown Reykjavík, when the clip-clop of stilettos marked chucking-out time from the nightclubs. I make my way to the fan park, located at the foot of the shallow lake that stretches south from the town hall.

When I get there, I find stoic early arrivers have settled on camping chairs and are taking shelter under umbrellas. Metal barriers separate an area to the right of the giant screen. This is where Tólfan – a vocal fan group that translates literally as 'twelve' – will set up their percussion. A man wearing a thick-shag jumper saunters through the barriers. A woolly Tólfan emblem is stitched across his chest. He holds his son in one hand and a carrier bag bulging with cans of lager in the other. Valuable cargo. While he greets his friends with thumping hugs, the screen cuts to Moscow.

On a hillside outside the Spartak Stadium, thousands of Icelanders bask in the sun. They hold their hands aloft. The first Viking clap of the day, the first of many. The sodden crowd in Reykjavík watch with a conflicting cocktail of pride and envy.

With 15 minutes until kick-off, the fanzone, tucked in a wooded hollow, is busy. A steady flow of people squelch through a gap in the trees and search for pockets of space in the crowd.

I stand beside the gazebo that shelters Tólfan's drums. Sandra and Rökkvi, her nine-year-old son, are to my right. They made a last-minute decision to drive through the lava fields from Keflavík to watch the match in the capital. Jon Faerber has come with them. At 6ft 4in and with dreadlocks down to his waist, he stands out. A ginger beard completes the image. An American approaches him.

'Man, you are the most Viking dude I've ever seen! Can I have a picture?'

Jon obliges, but disappoints his admirer when he opens his mouth to speak with an Australian drawl. He is a goalkeeper for Keflavík. A nomadic career has already taken Jon to Wales, Scotland, Germany, the USA and Chile. It is his second year in Iceland and his grasp of the language is improving. He is going native.

Four 20-something guys in front of us flash ankle beneath rolled-up jeans. One in a beige trench coat blows a plume of vape smoke into the air. It obscures the screen. His friend delivers the team news. 'Emil, Aron Einar, Gylfi ...' He refers to the players by first name, as is the custom in Iceland. The names betray Heimir Hallgrímsson's tactics. 'I don't have a magic formula,' he told the press when asked how he planned to stop Lionel Messi. He did, however, have a practical solution: to crowd the midfield and starve Messi of space, to suffocate him.

The camera switches to the tunnel in Moscow. The teams wait and fidget. They crick their necks. They clack their studs on the floor. They clear nasal passages with a finger over one nostril and a sharp outward snort.

Aron Gunnarsson, the captain, leans on the handles of a mascot's wheelchair. His ginger beard, grown for the tournament to adhere to the Viking stereotype, is striking against the blue of his tracksuit top. His calmness reassures. There is no testosterone or tub-thumping. Not outwardly, at least. Just the smile of a man who knows that the pressure rests on the shoulders of the opposition. The crowd around me are hushed, transfixed by the pixelated ball like children in the front row of a pantomime. The patter of raindrops on umbrellas creates a dignified applause.

Kick-off. The match falls into the pattern that most people anticipated. The battle between collective unit and star individual is a well-trodden trope in football. It is distilled into a pure form on the giant screen. Iceland organise and absorb. The Argentines ponder, pause, and pass to Messi.

Argentina are top-heavy; blessed with enviable attacking talent but a porous defence. Iceland create the better chances. Birkir Bjarnason drifts inside from the left flank, followed by his swishing blonde hair, and scuffs a shot just wide of the post. He winces. Everyone around me does the same.

Sergio Agüero is less profligate. On 19 minutes the squat striker cushions a lively pass and uses his low centre of gravity to pirouette away from Ragnar Sigurðsson. The defender barely has time to raise his leg before Agüero lashes a shot into the top corner. Reykjavík responds with puffed-out cheeks and eyebrows raised in acknowledgement of a simmering finish. Diego Maradona appears on screen, revelling in a corporate box. He balances a chunky cigar in his grin and ignores the 'no smoking' sign to his left.

But Diego only savours half a dozen puffs before Iceland draw level. Ravenous pressing leads to an error by Willy Caballero, the Argentine keeper. Alfreð Finnbogason is presented with a simple chance. From six yards he slots the ball between desperate limbs to become the first Icelander to score at a World Cup. Alfreð makes his way to a camera and screams something unintelligible into the lens. Nobody notices. The crowd around me have formed huddles and bounce to the irregular beat of pure jubilation. A man with creased eyes and greying temples stands separate from the flailing limbs of his companions, his gloved hands clasped behind his head. I watch him blink, as if he experiences the euphoria afresh each time he opens his eyes. His open mouth narrows to a disbelieving smirk. He joins the celebrating throng.

Half-time. A bleary-eyed man stumbles through the crowd, indiscriminately branding faces with red, white and blue paint. A tube of ash from his cigarette threatens to drop on to the sleeve of his knitted jumper. Another man delivers his assessment of the first half to a Netflix camera crew. 'It's going well, we just need to keep Messi quiet,' he says, holding his can of lager by the rim so it is out of shot.

The flecks of rain grow heavier. But it doesn't wash away the adrenaline. An aeroplane glides overhead on its way into Reykjavík airport. 'Áfram Ísland' is daubed on the underbelly. A football match – or any shared experience, for that matter – feels more momentous when you know that you are not just sharing it with those around you, but an entire country – even those in the sky. I feel as though Reykjavík is the centre of the world.

Argentina break the resistance after 54 minutes. Slippery Sergio Agüero sniffs out space in the penalty area and draws a foul from Hörður Björgvin Magnússon. Penalty. Spectators in Moscow watch through their iPhone screens as Messi places the ball on the spot and exhales, hands on hips. To my right, Sandra gives Rökkvi a piggyback so he can see above the plateau of heads that bob up and down like corks. Hannes Halldórsson fixes his eyes on Messi. He begins a plodding run-up, errs, and shoots meekly to the left. Hannes guesses the right way and swipes the ball clear.

Jon, the dreadlocked keeper, has lifted me up. Pandemonium. You experience a special type of joy when your team saves a penalty. A saved penalty is better than a goal because it comes moments after you have convinced yourself that your team has already conceded. And who better than Hannes to emerge as the hero? Rejected by a Third Division club when he was 22, semi-professional until he was 28. No matter what he does in the rest of his career, he will always have this moment.

The next 30 minutes crawl as the rain turns grass to mud. The saturated masses greet every tackle, save and clearance with baying defiance. Diego Maradona regains the attention of a cameraman to give light relief from the torture. He rubs his nose and his eyes widen. Nobody suspects hay fever.

Argentina's No. 10 scrambles desperately to atone for his penalty miss. The commentator repeats his name as he jinks into the Iceland box, each time with heightened panic. 'Messi, Messi, MESSI.' But even Messi, the best in the world, the man who blends football and ballet, cannot weave through the Icelandic stodge. The final minute of the match is a microcosm of the previous 89. Messi stands over a free kick on the edge of the box. Seconds remain. He shoots. The ball bounces back off the wall. The referee blows the full-time whistle. Messi thrashes the ball into the Moscow sky. Iceland sighs with relief.

People linger after the final whistle, as if the reality of what we have just watched only exists here and leaving will make it go away. People stay for the post-match interviews, aware that this moment will form a memory that lasts forever. Five years earlier, this moment was but a flicker in the eye of Iceland's most whimsical optimist.

Haffi leans back and catches my eye through the crowd. The match ended several hours ago but nobody wants the day to end. We had agreed to meet at Grandi Mathöll, a trendy food hall in an old harbourside warehouse. He and Anna have dressed up for the evening but the crowd contains a healthy smattering of blue nylon.

'Well, not bad,' he says through a wide grin. Anna shakes her head disbelievingly.

The evening passes quickly. Haffi delights in the Snapchat videos he took of himself during the match. They seem to consist of hyperventilation, nervous vaping and occasional dashes into the garden to release emotion. Now, after the excitement, it feels like Reykjavík has inhaled a substance that makes the body lighter and is a solvent for worry. Bleary-eyed revellers repeat 'Argentina' with a hard 'g'.

This has been a long time in the making.

## Chapter Two
# From gravel to grass

IN NOVEMBER 2013 Iceland lost to Croatia in a play-off to decide which nation would play at the World Cup in Brazil the following summer. It was the closest they had ever come. After the match Eiður Guðjohnsen lingered in front of the collage of sponsor logos. A journalist from RÚV, Iceland's state broadcaster, began the question that would hit Eiður like a punch in the stomach.

'You have delighted your nation for years. Started in the national team in 1996. The team's leading scorer. Will you continue in the national team?'

Eiður said nothing. He just blinked.

The first club in Iceland was formed in 1899 and became known as Knattspyrnufélag Reykjavíkur, graciously shortened to KR. A handful of other Reykjavík-based teams followed half a beat later. By 1912 there was enough interest for the inaugural league championship.

But while South American and European students soon learned to beat the aloof British masters at their own game, the progress of Icelandic football was rather more glacial. Frugal facilities shoulder some of the blame for this. The pitches – a term only applicable in a loose sense – were other-worldly rectangles of crushed lava. Before matches the local fire brigade would douse the black surface with water. It was then rolled to produce a bald tarmac effect. Touring sides from Britain – on whom Iceland relied for contact with the footballing world – treated the conditions with a haughty concoction of bemusement and disdain.

Icelanders had been playing football for a little over two decades when, in 1922, one such touring side travelled north, past the Shetlands and the Faroes, to Reykjavík. The Edinburgh Services Club played five matches against local opposition. The support was fervent. An aggregate crowd of 18,000 gathered for the spectacle – roughly equivalent to the entire adult population of Reykjavík. If they were ardent supporters of the local lads, the spectators had little to cheer about. The Edinburgh Services Club won all five matches. Twenty-eight goals scored. Zero goals conceded.

The tourists were often more concerned by the hospitality and scenery than sporting competition. John Couper was a member of the Aberdeen University football team that visited Iceland in 1937. 'We went to Iceland professedly to teach the Icelanders how to play football,' he wrote upon his return. 'But all we succeeded in teaching them was "Here's To The Good Old Whisky" and "One Man Went To Mow".'

While the threat of war escalated in mainland Europe through the 1930s, those with a sense of adventure continued to travel to Iceland. The Islington Corinthians, a rambling amateur outfit from North London, arrived in 1939. Over the previous two years the Corinthians had played 95 matches on four continents, in countries as disparate as Switzerland, Myanmar and Canada. They defeated an Iceland XI in Reykjavík and were presented with copies of *Iceland: Nature and Nation in Photographs* as a gift. Their Icelandic hosts were so eager to impress that they threw £10 worth of soap into the Great Geysir to ensure the natural cauldron was bubbling at maximum intensity.

The Corinthians travelled with the philanthropic intention of spreading the game of football. Iceland was the last stop on their journey. The club folded in 1940 after the escalation of the Second World War scuppered their plans for a tour of South Africa.

If the onset of war claimed Corinthians as a casualty, Icelandic football was a beneficiary. The British command recognised the strategic significance of Iceland's position in the North Atlantic and, desperate to deny the enemy a useful outpost, invaded the jagged coast on the morning of 10 May 1940. American troops arrived one year later. At their peak, the occupying forces numbered 30,000 – about 25 per cent of the Icelandic population. The sudden influx of Tommies and Yanks provided a significant boost to an economy that still relied on farming and fishing.

The cream of the British game served in the armed forces, and several distinguished footballers landed in Iceland. It was a cushy posting. The weather was a greater threat than the Wehrmacht. Football became one of the few ways to ease the boredom.

The *Midnight Sun*, a weekly newspaper for troops in Iceland, listed the line-ups from an intra-forces match in 1941. The following clubs had representatives on one team: Everton, Bolton, Newcastle, Doncaster, Blackpool and Fulham. And on the other team: Manchester United, Burnley, Middlesbrough, West Bromwich, Charlton and Carlisle. The war produced impossible combinations that could only exist in pub discussions and, nowadays, in fantasy football line-ups. They exposed Icelanders to elite football. The players navigating the lava pitches in 1940 were not hedonistic students from Scotland, but some of the best players in the Football League.

While it would be crass to overemphasise the positives of a forced occupation, the war was formative for Icelandic football.

The twinkle-toed troops played against the locals as well as between themselves. They even received the occasional shock, as an unnamed officer from Horncastle, Lincolnshire, explained in a letter home from 1940:

'We had another match versus the Icelanders. We again lost by the odd goal in three. We found the Icelanders very fast and skilful. When we first arrived they said: "Ah! The English. You must teach us how to play football." So we sent a scratch side along and they lost to their "pupils" by ten goals to nil. Since then we have been careful to pick the best team to meet them.'

Another member of the Lincolnshire Regiment – ostensibly the most diligent at writing home to their mothers – recalled an incident in a match against locals that made the British players 'gasp with amazement'. The Icelanders were awarded a penalty, but instead of 'giving it a good wham', the taker gently rolled the ball into the goalkeeper's arms. 'It seems from this,' the soldier deduced, 'that it's bad manners to score from the spot.'

This episode reveals much about a sporting tradition that began on the mottled pages of the Icelandic Sagas, a set of medieval texts that chronicle the settlers and the generations that came after them. Though the characters and their feuds are spiced with epic grandeur, the Sagas have a basis in fact.

The Saga writers describe crowds gathering on frozen lakes to watch names be made and honours lost through sport. These sports – the most popular of which, Knattleikr, bore a resemblance to Irish hurling – were underpinned by the importance of honour, fair play and acquitting oneself in the appropriate manner. These sporting values became pervasive as they passed from one generation to another, creating a moral thread that runs through Icelandic sport to the present day.

Flight Lieutenant Bernard Pead, from Portsmouth, also noticed a virtuous streak in Icelandic players. 'They are good lads and keen sportsmen and unfair ("dirty") play is not tolerated.'

Pead, however, was critical of crude Icelandic tactics. 'They are individually very skilful, but they just will not "work" the ball in an accepted British style,' he maligned. 'They tear all over the pitch and cover a lot of ground, but show a marked tendency to part with the ball readily and "balloon" it frequently. They would do well to follow our fundamental maxims of "keep the ball on the carpet" and "make the ball do the work".'

Pead served his assessment with lashings of irony. He disparaged the very characteristics that the rest of the world saw in British football. Indeed, seven decades after Pead's letter, Britain still struggles to sew those two 'fundamental maxims' into the fibre of the national game. Who knows how Icelandic football would have developed if Hungary – masters of the pass in the 1950s – had been the occupying force.

Nevertheless, the presence of British footballers nurtured Icelandic football at a time when enthusiasm was plentiful but experience scarce. International football beckoned.

'We do not expect to win matches, but only to gain experience at the hands of our English friends.'

Those were the servile words of Mr B. Schram, the manager of the Iceland team that travelled to Blitz-battered London in 1946 to play a series of amateur outfits, among them Dulwich Hamlet and a Representative XI from the Isthmian League. Iceland won one match out of five, against Ilford.

David Williams described 'a football lesson for Iceland' in the *Daily Herald*. He identified 'much dilly-dallying in the Icelandic rearguard' – written in earnestly innocent prose – as the reason for their downfall.

The same year, Iceland played their first FIFA-recognised fixture – a 0-3 defeat to former colonisers Denmark.

A maiden victory came in 1948 when Finland succumbed to a 2-0 loss in Reykjavík. And, in 1951, Iceland saw off Sweden 4-3, which was particularly impressive given the Swedes had reached the semi-final of the World Cup the previous year.

The first-ever coach of the Iceland national team was always half a beat ahead of his time. Freddie Steele was two months past his 30th birthday when he took charge of Iceland's inaugural fixture – that defeat to Denmark in Reykjavík. It was late in the summer of 1946 but still light enough to play football at midnight. The circumstances that led Steele to Iceland are unclear. We know that he spent the earlier summer months coaching KR in Reykjavík. What is clear, though, is that if luck had fallen in Steele's favour, he would have been assured of a place in the annals of English football history.

Steele was a prodigy ten years before he arrived in Iceland. He burst into the first team at Stoke City in 1934. He was 18 and this was an era in which such precocity was extremely rare. By his 21st birthday Steele was the top scorer in the First Division, with 33 goals in the 1936/37 season. In October 1936, he made his England debut at the age of 20. He was a rare talent, the rising star of English football.

The great Stanley Matthews starred in the same Stoke team. Matthews described Steele as 'lethal, clinical and merciless' in the box, and added evocatively that, 'Whenever the ball came to him, the reporters in the press box sharpened their pencils in anticipation.'

Then, in late 1937 as the sun was rising on Steele's peak years, his progress came to a halt with the jarring crack of a knee ligament. The severity of the injury was not lost on Steele. Bereft, he descended into depression. In 1939, at the age of 23, he announced his retirement.

The frayed ends in Steele's knee healed with time. His mental health also improved following hypnosis treatment. But if his capabilities as a footballer returned, so too did his rotten luck. Shortly after Steele took to the pitch again, the outbreak of the Second World War prompted the suspension of competitive fixtures. Events conspired to push him towards coaching.

Steele did not stay in Iceland for long. He returned to Stoke in 1946 as the Football League resumed after the war. His parting comment to *Morgunblaðið* was prescient: he predicted that Iceland would have a competitive team once grass pitches were available. He was right, in a way, although it was artificial grass rather than natural turf that coincided with Iceland's ascent.

Steele flourished when he became the manager of Port Vale in 1951. It is possible to say, with a mere pinch of hyperbole, that he revolutionised football tactics. For Steele has a strong claim to be the inventor of the 4-4-2 formation. The innovation came in the 1953/54 season. Port Vale – then of the lowly Third Division North – reached the semi-final of the FA Cup, losing narrowly to West Bromwich Albion, the eventual winners. Steele had already flaunted his tactical flair in the quarter-final against Blackpool, the incumbent champions featuring Stanley Matthews – the supple star of English football – on the wing.

The tactical orthodoxy in early-1950s England was the 'WM' formation created by Herbert Chapman in response to the relaxed offside rule introduced in 1925. Within that system, two wingers hugged the touchline and waited to be fed. Steele changed that. In training ahead of the quarter-final against Blackpool, Steele instructed one of his wingers to imitate Matthews, so his midfield and defence could practise blunting his threat in a dress rehearsal.

'Freddie was a clever man tactically,' Harry Poole, a member of the 1953/54 Port Vale squad, told the *Stoke Sentinel* in 2014. 'In fact, it was him who introduced wingers tracking back. Colin Askey and Dickie Cunliffe both did it under him in the 53/54 semi-final team – long before England did it to win the World Cup in 1966.'

The Port Vale players venerated their coach. 'Freddie Steele was light years ahead of anybody,' Graham Barnett, who joined Vale in 1954, added. 'In 1953/54 we played with two up, four across the middle, four across the back.'

The 4-4-2 was born. Ironically, Steele barely saw his tactical child in action during its finest hour. He usually stalked the touchline with a tweed trilby on his head and a metal ring from his son's tent in his hand but, while Vale outmanoeuvred Blackpool, he was in the dressing-room bath with a towel wrapped around his head. The pressure was too much.

Steele preached the primacy of collective organisation at a time when the prevailing approach to football was to let the talented players get on with being talented. He subverted accepted ideas about how the game should be played, and as a result Port Vale were impenetrable that season. They won the league title with ostentatious ease, by a record margin of 11 points. Even more remarkably, Vale conceded just 21 goals in 46 league games.

The immovable Vale defence became known as the 'Iron Curtain'. Incidentally, a man on the other side of the east–west divide is credited with inventing the 4-4-2. In his book *Inverting the Pyramid: A History of Football Tactics*,

Jonathan Wilson cites Viktor Maslov as the first man to use the formation, at Dynamo Kiev in the mid-1960s. Maslov undoubtedly came up with the idea independently. He would have been unaware of the tactical nuances of a provincial English club, especially at a time when the flow of information across Europe was limited. But he was not the first. Freddie Steele was a decade ahead of him.

The 4-4-2 formation became ubiquitous in Britain. It also spread to unexpected people and places. *Africa United* is a documentary about a cosmopolitan lower-league team in Iceland. The players come from all over the world. Some are in Iceland to find work, others to escape war. A Guinean named Cheick Bangoura stars in one delightfully surreal scene. On the long journey back from an away match, Cheick seizes the microphone and makes the aisle of the bus his stage. He embarks on a meandering motivational speech. The highlight comes when he announces, in a thick west-African imitation of Mike Bassett, 'We play four-four-fuckin'-two.'

The first star of Icelandic football stands on a plinth outside Laugardalsvöllur. Albert Guðmundsson's poise is captured in the shadowy curves of a bronze statue. He was the first professional footballer from Iceland and the first to forge a career outside his home country.

Albert's early life was typical of a time when Iceland was not a place of plenty. His family was poor. One of seven children, he was forced to live with his grandmother when he was 12 following the death of his father.

Albert played briefly for Rangers while studying in Glasgow, before moving south to join Arsenal as an amateur. The wiry, high-cheeked Icelander impressed for the Gunners. He grasped the limelight in an exhibition match against Sparta Prague in 1946, but work permit issues in England pushed Albert towards a glamorous yet nomadic career on the continent. Nancy was his first stop. Then came AC Milan and Racing Club de Paris. He scored at a commendable rate of a goal every other game across three seasons in the French capital, before a spell on the south coast with Nice completed his European tour.

Albert moved into politics after retirement, serving as a prominent member of the Alþingi – the Icelandic parliament – and even standing for election in the 1980 presidential election. Latterly, he returned to France as the Ambassador to Iceland, where he enjoyed the title of Monsieur Guðmundsson.

Albert's son, Ingi Björn Albertsson, is in his sixties now. 'He was at that age when football was more or less beginning in Iceland,' Ingi Björn says with Nordic lollop. 'There was nobody before him. He had a great career. I think everyone looked up to him and so did we, his children. We wanted to go in the same direction.'

Ingi Björn did follow his father's peculiar path. He won 15 caps for Iceland in the 1970s before entering politics. Indeed, football bounced off every branch of the family tree. Ingi Björn's daughter, Kristbjörg Ingadóttir, played for the women's national team. Her son – named Albert Guðmundsson after his great-grandfather, to whom he bears a startling resemblance – played fleetingly for Iceland at the 2018 World Cup.

The details of the original Albert Guðmundsson's career have faded into the mists of time. Albert spoke little of football once he was in the political sphere. A scrapbook of clippings from *L'Équipe*, the French sports daily, is all that remains in the family.

'It's a shame that there are not so many videos from that time,' Ingi Björn muses. 'I'm told he was a technical, quick player with a good head. You would call him a playmaker today.'

Albert played for Iceland until 1958. The national team survived on a gruelly diet of friendly matches against fellow Nordic nations, garnished with amateur representatives of England, Scotland, Wales and Ireland. It was a cosy circuit with few surprises. Icelandic clubs, meanwhile, received a shock when the nascent European Cup pitted them against Europe's best.

Reykjavík was the setting for Liverpool's first-ever match in the European Cup. Bill Shankly's side faced KR in August 1964. The venerated Boot Room tactician enjoyed the trip, not least because beer was illegal in Iceland at the time and he could let his team out on the town without fear of the consequences. Presumably the Liverpool players did not find the spirits, as they were rampant. 0-5 was the score in the first leg.

'Dismissed with the casual air of swatting a fly,' was Frank McGhee's scathing appraisal in the *Daily Mirror*. 'There seems very little point in holding the second leg at Anfield.'

The worst was yet to come. 1967 was the nadir of Icelandic football. In August of that year the national team suffered a 14-2 mauling at the hands of Denmark.

The political context intensified the humiliation. Iceland gained independence from Denmark in 1944. Yet a precious collection of medieval Icelandic manuscripts – a vital part of the nation's proud literary heritage – remained under lock and key in Copenhagen. The manuscripts became a significant point of contention and the matter went to the Danish courts, which ruled that the manuscripts must be sent back to Iceland. Children were given the day off school to attend a sombre ceremony as the first set of manuscripts arrived on a Danish frigate in 1971, a gesture which smoothed the relationship between coloniser and colony.

At the time of the 14-2 embarrassment, however, diplomacy was terse.

Later in 1967, Icelandic football slipped into a state of gloom that verged on existential crisis. Aberdeen beat KR 10-0 in the Cup Winners' Cup to induce the malaise. The presence of Jens Petersen – a Dane – in the Aberdeen team intensified the shame.

Sveinn Jónsson, the KR coach, delivered a rather melodramatic response. 'The whole question of our participation in European competitions will have to be considered by the club,' he said.

A decade later things were looking up. Iceland's 1-0 victory over Northern Ireland in 1977 meant that for the first time, they had won a World Cup qualification match. They savoured it; *Morgunblaðið* showed the goal from three angles the following morning.

Alongside that elusive first qualification victory, Iceland began to produce genuinely elite players. Ásgeir Sigurvinsson won the Bundesliga with Stuttgart in 1984 and secured a place in the Team of the Year at the end of the season.

Arnór Guðjohnsen was the next star to adorn bedroom walls. There is a story, possibly apocryphal, that he piqued the interest of Sampdoria after facing the Italian side for Anderlecht in the final of the 1990 Cup Winners' Cup. Paolo Mantovani, the club president, arranged a deal but backed out at a late stage, instead deciding to keep Toninho Cerezo, the Brazil international, in the squad. He reasoned that if Guðjohnsen failed, people would question why he signed an Icelandic player. Sticking with a Brazilian, with all the samba and Copacabana cache that entailed, was a safer reputational bet. Guðjohnsen joined Bordeaux instead, while Sampdoria went on to win Serie A the following season, for the first and only time in the club's history.

Víðir Sigurðsson, the sports editor of *Morgunblaðið* and a veteran journalist, believes the most talented Icelandic players passed through the national team in the 1980s.

'The funny thing,' he says, 'is that if I had to choose Iceland's best ever team, very few of the current players would be in it. We had really good players between 1980 and 1990, but the rest of the team was filled with amateurs. They always lacked a little edge.'

Víðir identifies the late 1980s as a watershed. 'It was before the 1990 World Cup that Iceland, for the first time, seemed to have a chance of doing something. It has slowly started to change since then.'

Iceland finished bottom of their qualification group for Italia '90, but that did not tell the full story. They were only three points behind Austria, who progressed in second place behind the Soviet Union. The qualification campaign for Euro '92 affirmed that Iceland were no longer goal-difference fodder like San Marino or Malta. In the '92 campaign Iceland beat Spain 2-0 in Reykjavík and only lost one match by a margin greater than one goal: a 3-1 defeat to France in Paris. It was the start of the second age of Icelandic football: the nearly years.

The 1990s and early 2000s was a period of inconsistency, as Iceland struggled to carry momentum from one qualification campaign to another. In qualification for the 1994 World Cup, Iceland finished behind Greece and Russia with a creditable tally of eight points from eight games. Yet in the next round of qualifiers, for Euro '96, they floundered at the bottom of the group, and the only victories in their limp effort to reach the 1998 World Cup came against lowly Liechtenstein.

This ragged pattern continued. Iceland were unbeaten in their first six qualifiers for Euro 2000, including a 1-1 draw against a France side that would go on to win the tournament in Rotterdam. The following edition of the competition, held in Portugal in 2004, was Iceland's best opportunity for tournament football. With Eiður Guðjohnsen outscoring everyone else in the qualification group, Iceland finished just one point behind Scotland, who progressed to the play-offs.

The campaign for Euro 2008 reflected the frailties that dogged Iceland throughout this period. It took a late goal by Andrés Iniesta to salvage a 1-1 draw for Spain in Reykjavík. Yet Iceland also lost 3-0 to Liechtenstein. They produced some excellent performances but were incapable of doing so on a consistent basis.

Iceland were more familial than formidable in a match against Estonia in 1996. A first-half hat-trick by Bjarki

Gunnlaugsson meant they were three goals to the good when the fourth official shuffled to the touchline to send on a substitute. These were the days before electronic substitute boards. The official held a placard embossed with '9' in his left hand and another placard with '13' in his right. '9' trotted to the side of the pitch and embraced his replacement, who looked faintly embarrassed as he swerved a kiss on the cheek and took his place in attack. Eiður Guðjohnsen, aged 17, replaced his father Arnór, 34.

Despite the tenderness of the moment, Eiður regrets that he never shared the pitch with his father. Allegedly, the Icelandic Football Association (KSÍ) wanted to play them together in Reykjavík, where the event would generate more attention, but fate intervened in an under-18s match. This is an excerpt from *Inside the Volcano*, a documentary that followed Iceland's qualification campaign for Euro 2016. In Eiður's words:

'I remember one moment. We were walking down the steps and I said as a joke: "What if I broke my leg?" I never forget it. It was just something I said. Then it happened the next day in the game. It was surreal. As soon as I was tackled I heard and felt something go. The first thing I thought was: "Damn, the game with Dad. Gone."'

Fast-forward 17 years from that day in Estonia, to the aftermath of the play-off defeat to Croatia. Eiður had more meat on his cheekbones in 2013, but his blonde hair had thinned and receded.

He pondered the question at the top of this chapter: was that the closing scene of his international career? His silence drew the camera zoom like a magnetic force.

While his club career with Chelsea and Barcelona yielded domestic and European titles, Iceland had never tasted tournament football.

Eiður searched for words that he could not find. He fiercely massaged his furrowed brow.

The residual amateurism in Iceland must have contrasted with life at Pep Guardiola's Barcelona. In 2007, shortly after Eiður joined Barça from Chelsea, Iceland played Spain in Majorca. Eiður and his team-mates walked to training in complimentary hotel slippers, before changing into boots sourced from a local sports shop. The reason? Their equipment had gone missing during the journey.

Eiður's eyes were blotchy. Twenty-two seconds after the question, he spluttered a trembled answer.

'I'm ... I'm very afraid that this was my last game for the national team.'

'Thank you for everything,' the interviewer said. They embraced a manly embrace, with backslapping and taut biceps.

It was not his last game. In fact, he would wear the blue shirt a further ten times. Sixty-seven years after Iceland's inaugural match, the good times were coming.

# Chapter Three
## Facilities

SOME STRANDS of this story have curious beginnings, far away from Iceland. One such strand is that of Tom Dent, an Englishman in the depths of Norway.

Tom crouches on his haunches as the four goalkeepers under his tutelage begin the week with a high-intensity drill. The LED clock mounted high on the wall of Nordlandshallen – a cavernous indoor football pitch – reveals the time in red speckles: 8.33 on a Monday morning. Tom is a youth coach at Bodø/Glimt, recently promoted to the Norwegian First Division. Raised in the south of England, he never imagined that football would take him to Bodø, 60 miles inside the Arctic Circle.

Two keepers shimmy around the back of a training dummy and save a shot. Every pass and parry echoes like a round of distant artillery fire. Tom arranges a GoPro camera on a small tripod. He records the goalkeepers as they stutter on the balls of their feet and dive. He will later dissect the footage and upload it to a shared drive. The goalkeepers will analyse their stance and positioning. Tom only suggests improvements during the drill if a keeper has conceded several goals in a row. They are less inclined to absorb advice if they have made a string of saves. They see no reason to change.

On the other side of a canvas partition, a segment of the hall is unlit. A shard of morning sun breaks through the frame of the fire exit. A teenage boy trains alone. It is mild inside but he wears a black snood that covers his neck. He forms a square with four cones and waits, poised, with a ball at his feet. A glance down at his watch and he goes, scampering around the right-angled assault course. He kneads and caresses the ball. The chase lasts for 30 seconds. The lone dribbler puts his palms on his knees and heaves air into his lungs. Clockwise. Anticlockwise. Repeat.

Training takes place indoors because the weather is football's enemy in these parts. The day before, Bodø/ Glimt hosted Lillestrøm in the opening match of the season. Snow began to fall five minutes before kick-off. The players formed tracks and patterns in the snow, as if a leash of mountain foxes had been scurrying about. The pitch markings disappeared completely after 30 minutes. Both teams shuffled down the tunnel as two tractors erased the heat maps they had left in the cold.

One mile from the Nordlandshallen, along a slushy road, Aasmund Bjørkan sits in the glass-panelled offices below the main stand of Glimt's stadium. He is Bodø born and raised. He played for the club, managed the club, and now his son, Fredrik, is the first-team left-back.

Aasmund is eager to emphasise the influence football has on Bodø, and the perception of the town across the country. The United Nations has criticised Norway's treatment of the indigenous Sámi people concentrated in the north of the Scandinavian peninsula. Bodø does not have a significant Sámi population but still felt the effects of discrimination.

'The first big period for Bodø/Glimt was in 1975,' Aasmund explains, 'when we broke through in Norwegian football. Back then it was almost like apartheid here. If you came from northern Norway you couldn't rent an apartment in Oslo. We were looked down upon. Then along came this extremely good team and they changed the whole perception of people from the north. It was like the '68 generation, flower power!'

Aasmund is in his forties. He does not remember the ambassadors of 1975. But he leans back and puffs out his cheeks when I ask about the football house on the other side of town.

'The Nordlandshallen means an enormous amount for me, for the club and for football in this region,' he says, choosing his words deliberately. 'When the Nordlandshallen came it was a revolution.'

The Nordlandshallen was built in 1991, when Glimt were moping in the Third Division. By 1993, they had won the Norwegian Cup, had two consecutive promotions and had finished as runners-up in the First Division. The northerners, playing a portion of their home fixtures in the Nordlandshallen, completed an assault on the upper echelons of Norwegian football.

Europe was next. Sampdoria travelled to Bodø in 1994 in the first round of the Cup Winners' Cup. They tasted defeat by a scoreline of 3-2. The Italian side won the second leg 2-0 to progress to the next round, but Glimt had already achieved more than they could have imagined, and that was largely down to improved facilities.

'That shows what happened in the three years after the Nordlandshallen came,' Aasmund says. 'From January '92 to '94, we went from being a level-three club to beating Sampdoria. It was many things: a good coach, good players ... but the Nordlandshallen was the key driver. We were more or less invincible when we played there.'

The start of Aasmund's career coincided with Glimt's rise. He owes a lot to the Nordlandshallen. So does the lone dribbler bamboozling cones on a Monday morning. And so too does Icelandic football.

It is April 2018 and a little over a year has passed since Geir Þorsteinsson stepped down as the president of the KSÍ. He held the position for ten years until Guðni Bergsson – the former Tottenham Hotspur and Bolton Wanderers defender – took over in early 2017. But his involvement with the KSÍ began in the 1980s. He has seen the changing epochs of Icelandic football from the inside.

'I would have been elected no problem,' Geir insists as a coffee machine rasps in a room at the end of the KSÍ's offices at Laugardalsvöllur. Geir is no longer in charge, but he still feels like part of the furniture. The draw for the Icelandic Cup is about to take place and I wait, nodding and smiling at the appropriate moments, as Geir jokes with the fixtures manager. 'When you've been there for so long, you know everyone,' he says jovially.

It was the burgeoning Guðjohnsen clan of footballers who, unknowingly, signalled to Geir that it was time to give someone else a chance.

'I worked with Arnór Guðjohnsen and I was there when Eiður came on for his father in Estonia in 1996. Now Eiður has quit and his son is playing with the under-19s. I thought, "Wow, I'm now working with the third generation of this family!"'

A Monopoly box occupies the table next to us. It is fitting that a board game based on property development will eavesdrop our conversation. Geir's legacy in Icelandic football will be the infrastructure he leaves behind.

'When I was young,' he begins, 'we had two or three months on the gravel and then maybe three months on natural grass. In the winter we had frozen gravel, snow, or we could run on the streets.'

Decades in football administration have not dulled his frothing enthusiasm for the game. He barely finishes one sentence before the next one begins. 'Coaching the youth was difficult,' he adds, 'sometimes impossible. The crazy thing with the climate is not the cold, as many people think. It's the wind. It's so windy. It's difficult to do technical training.'

Conscious of the limitations of their environment, Icelanders flicked envious glances back across to the facilities in Norway. Journalists gushed in *Morgunblaðið* about the team from Bodø that had catapulted through the divisions after building an indoor football house. More broadly, the Norway national team was flourishing under the pragmatic hand of Egil 'Drillo' Olsen and his statistics-driven brand of efficient football. Norwegian football seemed like a hub of innovation. Iceland became curious.

'In the early 1990s we heard that Norway had built one or two football houses,' Geir says. 'We sent a delegation over to Bodø. We sent them to look at the Nordlandshallen and study it. We thought, "This is the future for our football game."'

Armed with that conviction, the KSÍ got to work. 'In cooperation with all the local councils in Iceland we held a congress and said: "This is the future of football in Iceland: artificial and covered." We made our own vision. We used Bodø and made our own template. We made our own brochure on how the houses should look and how we wanted it to happen. How many full-size houses? How many half-size houses? Where should they be distributed around Iceland?'

It is reasonable to refer to a football-house 'revolution', so rapid was the pace of change. The first full-size football house appeared in Keflavík in 2000. Six more sprung up across Iceland in the next eight years, as well as six half-size structures. They look like military hangars from a sci-fi film set, wedged in place by banks of grass that slope up to the roof. Some football houses, like the one in Akranes, are open all day for kids to come and go. All of them reverberate with muffled shouts and the woolly thud of boot on ball that creates a swelling urge to join in.

The KSÍ timed the campaign well. 'Luckily for us, our economy started booming,' Geir says with the smile of someone who knows what followed. 'Nobody knows how we did it and there was nothing behind it. It ended with the financial crisis in 2008. But we really enjoyed riding this.'

Between 2003 and 2008, newly privatised Icelandic banks borrowed over $140 billion, a figure almost ten times the country's Gross Domestic Product. A small band of insatiable investors embarked on an international spending binge. During a match between Iceland and Denmark in the mid-2000s, the Icelandic supporters aimed a tongue-in-cheek chant at their former colonisers. 'We're coming for Tivoli next,' they goaded. Tivoli Gardens is an ornate amusement park in the heart of Copenhagen and a site of cultural importance for Danes. It was like Iceland playing the United States and singing about buying Mount Rushmore.

I ask Geir what would have happened if the *kreppa* – and the Weimar-esque inflation that followed – had happened five years earlier. 'It would have been devastating,' he says unequivocally. The investment in football facilities would have been impossible without the cash and confidence swilling around Iceland.

The KSÍ used television revenue and funds from UEFA to stabilise its own financial position through the 1990s. Yet the local councils paid for the football houses. 'We were clever in approaching politicians,' Geir trumpets. 'They have children and they want the best facilities for their children. It was always like this. We tried to convince them to build facilities for their own children, because if politicians see gain for themselves ...' Geir would know. In May 2018 he narrowly lost out in the mayoral election for his home town of Kópavogur.

Football facilities became the must-have social investment. No politician wanted the neighbouring town to nudge ahead in the artificial-turf arms race. And, crucially, the KSÍ was preaching to the converted when it came to the benefits for young people of participation in sport.

In 1992 two academics at the University of Iceland – Rúnar Vilhjálmsson and Þórólfur Þórlindsson – published

the results of a questionnaire they had sent to 1,200 15-
and 16-year-olds across the country. The study revealed
alarming levels of alcohol and tobacco consumption among
the respondents. Amid the hand-wringing, however, the
study presented a solution. It showed that adolescents who
participated in strenuous exercise smoked and drank less
and showed fewer signs of depression and anxiety. The
same strand of research continued throughout the 1990s,
and the publication of each paper added weight to the idea
that participation in organised sports had positive social
and developmental effects on young Icelanders.

Iceland, like Norway, is a social democracy. Politicians
try to give all citizens the chance to play sport, learn a
musical instrument, dance, or pursue whatever activity
integrates them in society and keeps them off street
corners. This attitude has deep roots. An Englishman
called J. Wishart visited Iceland in 1935 and wrote the
following in the *Sunderland Echo* about his visit to a football
club: 'Every encouragement is given to youth, and training
exists any day for any members of the public who wish to
participate.'

Jarred by the prevalence of teenage hedonism in the
1990s and guided by an emerging academic consensus
in favour of community-level sports for all, Iceland
was particularly receptive to the benefits of large-scale
investment in sports facilities. That endured in 2018. 'If
you keep kids active in organised sports, you'll have better
health outcomes for them,' Kári Jónsson – the head of
sports and recreation for Garðabær, an affluent town to
the south of Reykjavík – told *TIME*. 'It is not just physical
health,' he added, 'but mental and social too. That's why

everything pays back into the community.' At the time of the interview, work was poised to begin on a $40m football house in Garðabær.

Geir has no time for false modesty. He is openly proud of his part in the football-house revolution. But he is even prouder of a parallel development that happened alongside it.

'In 2004 we made our own mini-pitch project, which was also very important for the game. The emphasis was on building mini-pitches at schools. Footballers, clubs or the public could use them after school hours. But during school hours the children could play football there. It was unbelievable. And quick, too. We built them in two or three years.'

The mini-pitches are easy to identify. Whether nestled in the folds of the eastern fjords, alongside volcanoes in the south, or in the concrete bleakness of suburban Reykjavík, they are identical: five-a-side arenas clad with wood and decorated with sponsor logos above each goal. Two things are striking: the absence of vandalism and the total openness. There are no fences, no boundaries, nothing to stop children wandering in or out.

'It was possible because of clever planning,' Geir continues. 'UEFA gave us a gift because they were celebrating 50 years. They gave every association one million Swiss francs, or something. I don't remember exactly. With that we could build 20 pitches. But we got sponsors. Big sponsors.

'We said, "Come on, join us, let's build 40 pitches." Every company in Iceland wanted to sponsor one. We also got some extra grants from the government and the private sector. We managed to build 110 pitches. Again, that was cleverly done. We made a brochure and sent it to the councils. We said, "If we give you the grass and bring in workers from abroad to lay it, you build the frame."'

Geir omits the cleverest part of all. During the long winters, when all around is white, geothermal energy keeps many of the mini-pitches green. In Reykjavík 99.9 per cent of properties are heated by scalding water that rises from the earth. Most of the waste water – that which is unused by houses – heats the streets in the centre of town. The rest keeps mini-pitches around the capital free from snow.

The futuristic novelty of indoor football funnels attention in the direction of the football houses. They have become an object of fascination for anyone seeking to unpick Iceland's success. Yet through sheer numbers – there are now 154 in Iceland – the mini-pitches play a bigger role. They serve the same purpose as the courts and cages of South London or the irregular pockets of asphalt in the favelas above Rio de Janeiro. The mini-pitches are a blank canvas for Icelandic children. The children can express themselves and be spontaneous with a football. They learn the creative side of the game away from a structured environment. They can mix it with the older kids. They can practise and then practise some more.

The writer Malcolm Gladwell frequently returns to the '10,000-hour rule' in his book *Outliers*. The principle – based on a 1993 study by Anders Ericsson – is that it takes, on average, 10,000 hours of deliberate practice to become an expert in a given field. Talent is a product of graft. Some academics criticise the 10,000-hour rule as a crude oversimplification, yet the basic premise is hard to dispute: people get significantly better at something if they practise it a lot. The mini-pitches – and, to a lesser extent, the football houses – transformed football from a summer pastime in Iceland to an all-year sport and provided a practice space that did not previously exist.

'That was an important step,' Geir says of the dinky pitches that have become Petri dishes for fermenting football talent. 'In a decade, we changed our conditions from really bad to very good. You could, perhaps, say excellent.'

The hyperbole is justified. According to KSÍ figures in 2018, there are 23,000 registered footballers in Iceland. Those players share 179 full-size pitches – a mix of indoor and outdoor, natural and artificial. Adding the mini-pitches and half-size pitches gives a grand total of 333 facilities, which roughly equates to one for every 67 registered players.

Geir leans towards me. 'I had a clear vision. I always have a clear vision of where I want to go in football. I said to people, "One day we will go to a final tournament." They replied, "Yeah, yeah. Dream on." The media guys were laughing at me. So were handball. They said, "You're football and you'll never get anywhere." I had to work hard on this. We had to improve the infrastructure: the houses and the artificial pitches. And then we could develop the game.'

Before rectangles of artificial turf interrupted the rock, Icelanders went to extreme measures to play football. One well-known family was at the radical end of this spectrum.

Ólafur Már Sigurðsson leans against a shimmering cream kitchen surface. His parents' apartment in Hafnarfjörður overlooks the harbour. It is window weather, as they say in Iceland: sunny but cold. The showroom floors and minimalist furniture leave no doubt that this is a shoes-off-at-the-door household. Óli is ten years older than his brother Gylfi, Iceland's best player. Óli has larger saddlebags beneath his eyes. His cheeks are fuller. Apart from that, the brothers are identical.

Óli was once a promising golfer. He played a few European Tour events but never made a breakthrough. Beyond the telescope on the balcony and the German liner in the harbour, the light-green shades of a links course peep around the headland. 'That's where I played,' he says. 'It's pretty cool. The fairways follow the flow of the lava field.'

Alongside golf, Óli concentrated on moulding his younger brother into a professional footballer. One winter in the late 1990s, their father rented a warehouse so Óli had a space to coach Gylfi.

'We had to do it,' Óli says earnestly. 'In those days there were no artificial indoor halls and we couldn't train anywhere in the wintertime. So he rented this warehouse. We could go to kick the ball around, practise ball control, receiving the ball ... It helped. We went there many times.'

He appreciates that option was closed to most people. 'You have to be financially strong. Our dad always had money. He wasn't *very* rich or something, but he put all his money into his sons, Gylfi and me. You also have to be a little bit crazy, and our dad is a little bit crazy.'

Óli pauses to think. 'He played darts for the Iceland team, but he injured his wrist and he couldn't throw anymore. So he started throwing with his left hand. He practised and practised until he was back in the national team.' Óli smiles to himself and wryly shakes his head, pleased that he has found an anecdote to illustrate his father's eccentricity. He rarely mentions his mother or half-sister. Gylfi was a project for the men of the house. It started when he was six or seven.

The aim was to make Gylfi a classical midfielder who relied on cerebral attributes rather than athleticism. 'He was so slow and weak that most people here didn't think he was going anywhere,' Óli recalls. 'But we think that technique wins in the end. You can be fast but there is no point in running fast if you don't know what to do with the ball. We realised that this guy was never going to be fast. He was never going to be the strongest. So we said, "OK, he has to have something different."'

Óli devoured coaching literature. When he identified a suitable drill, he would run through it himself to make sure he could explain it to Gylfi. Óli also used his golfers' eye for meticulous technique. He recorded Gylfi on a clunky camcorder and spent hours editing the footage into clips so his younger brother could digest what he had done well and what he needed to improve.

Meanwhile, Gylfi followed the football houses. As a 14-year-old he left FH, his local side, for Breiðablik.

'FH didn't have any facilities,' Óli says. 'The artificial grass was crap. It was like the road, it was so hard. It was dangerous and he was actually weak in the knees after a few training sessions. Breiðablik had recently built an indoor house so he went there and stayed for just over two years until he joined Reading.'

Did Óli worry about pushing his brother too hard? 'A little bit. At the time I was reading about how to avoid going over the limit. When he was very young – seven to ten years old – I was always acting the silly guy. I would be the goalkeeper and let him shoot and have fun. But at the same time he was also doing drills. I was tricking him into it. And then, when he was really having fun and laughing, I took him home. He was like, "Can we stay and do one more?" I would say, "No, no, no, let's go," so when he got home he would have this feeling that he wanted to go back.'

I knew about Gylfi's childhood training regime before meeting Óli. It did not sit easily with me. The prevailing narrative around 'pushy parents' is negative. It has become synonymous with a lack of empathy. But I feel placated after an hour in Óli's company. The family pushed Gylfi, but did so with tenderness and logic. When he moved to Reading as a 16-year-old, both parents moved to England to smooth the transition. Naturally, people still titter and gossip, but Óli does not mind.

'If you're just like the average Joe, that's fine. But you're not going to stand out. It's the different people who succeed more than the average, normal people. We always tried to think outside the box.'

Óli coaches his own sons now. His 11-year-old is like Gylfi: tall, languid and technical. His seven-year-old is nippy and a quick learner. He does not have to rent a warehouse for them to play football in the winter. Things have changed for the better. Yet Óli thinks the impact of new facilities is overstated.

'A lot of people say Iceland are successful now because they built all these indoor houses and artificial pitches.

But I don't see it. It helps with technique but it's not the reason. It's played a role but it's a lot deeper. Take all these guys in the national team now. Who is challenging them? There is nobody coming up. If the indoor houses were such a huge thing, the guys in the team should have younger guys challenging them.'

Common sense suggests that as facilities in Iceland improve, better footballers will emerge. But Óli is not alone in questioning this assumption. Some people in Iceland deny that better facilities will improve the standard of the national team. In fact, they argue that extra resources may work like an inverse-U curve and make things worse once a certain point is reached.

Young footballers faced a paucity of footballing resources 20 years ago. They played on gravel. The wind numbed their cheeks. Yet those conditions forced footballers to develop discipline and fortitude to compensate for a lack of technical prowess. Many identify these mental attributes as key to Iceland's success, but will they become dormant as children migrate to plush facilities? Heimir Hallgrímsson entered the Iceland set-up as assistant to Lars Lagerbäck in 2011 and became joint-manager in 2014, before leading Iceland to the World Cup as the sole manager. He fears the answer is 'yes'.

'That character is created in the cold and gravel,' he says. 'I'm afraid it could disappear. To be a footballer back then, you needed to be a little tougher than they are today. One of the reasons why Icelanders have been considered a little bit tougher is because we had to endure playing football in bad weather, in the cold and the wind.

'Hopefully we can keep that mentality and speciality in the future. That's something that we, the coaches, have to put in our coach education. We have to focus more on how we would like the Iceland national team players to be. Abroad you can probably find players with more speed and technique. So we have to have the characters. We have to praise the characters. They have to be the ones who, in the end, will be the national team players.'

Þorgrímur Þráinsson, a former international footballer turned author, expressed similar concerns to sociologist Viðar Halldórsson in the book *Sport in Iceland*.

'The football halls are very good for making sure people feel comfortable at practices and can work on their technique and so on. But they take away the experience of being out in the rain and wind and snow, and playing on gravel, and the need to be tough and never give up. Things have got a lot softer. I'm afraid that going soft like this could make us end up in a bad way.'

Heimir and Þorgrímur's comments reflect a moist-eyed fetishisation of hardship that Icelanders often dabble in, particularly members of the generation that bridges the gap between old and new. Take Þorgrímur as an example. His mother was born in a turf house in an era when scarcity was a motivator and stoicism was venerated. His son, by contrast, has grown up in a consumerist society in which the majority want for little. To many Icelanders, football houses represent a different set of values to the ones they grew up with. They represent snugness over struggle. That is unfamiliar territory in the North Atlantic and it plays up to hazy concerns about social decline and a losing battle against video games and smartphones.

A suspicion of comfort is not exclusive to Iceland. Stephen Francis is the co-founder of the MVP Track and Field Club in Kingston, Jamaica. The MVP began in 1999 and by 2016 its athletes had won 27 Olympic medals. Asafa Powell and Shelly-Ann Fraser-Pryce are among the sprinters to have passed through the club. Yet the facilities are frugal. The fastest people in the world hang their jackets on a mesh fence before training on spiky, yellowing grass.

Francis never upgraded the facilities because, as he rather cryptically puts it to Rasmus Ankersen in *The Gold Mine Effect*, 'The most important thing a man has to tell you is what he's not telling you.' Francis gauges newcomers' reactions to the facilities and uses them as a test of character. It helps him separate those who are motivated by comfortable surroundings from those who are driven by a deeper desire to succeed.

The difference between Iceland and Kingston is one of necessity versus desire. Athletes in Kingston can do the same training whether the facilities are basic or lavish. Their comfort may vary, but they can still train. In Iceland, however, there is nowhere to train in the winter without artificial pitches. Nor is there anywhere to educate coaches.

Sceptics repeat that the players who took Iceland to the Euros and World Cup did not develop in the football houses. It is a fair point. Most of that cohort were outside during their formative years of technical development because indoor facilities had not yet been built.

Jóhann Berg Guðmundsson was one of few players of his generation to benefit from the improved facilities. 'I was in the big indoor hall at Breiðablik,' he recalls. 'I was young, probably about 12 or 13. I would literally spend more time there than at my home, just kicking a ball. I started to know the guys in the first team. Then, one time, they needed an extra player and asked me. I was small, but really quick and technical.'

Jóhann Berg does not agree that pristine facilities will blunt Iceland's edge. 'It depends on how strong you are in here,' he says, tapping his forefinger against his temple. 'You can see that with our group, we are really strong in our heads. You need that as a professional. I don't think having an indoor hall would take that out of you. You're training with better facilities and it should be better for you ... if you have the right mindset.'

It is too early to tell if the echoing football houses and mini-pitches will adversely affect a perceived Icelandic toughness. But that conjecture is probably a manifestation of two things. First, the back-in-my-day condescension that each generation invariably reserves for those who follow. It is the same reflex that causes us to inwardly tut when we see a family in a restaurant and all the children are swiping smartphones. Second, an internal tension among some Icelanders, who are reluctant to confine tradition to the past, yet have a fierce sense of national pride and do not want to see Iceland left in the wake of other, more innovative, nations.

A break from tradition may be a good thing if that tradition consisted of playing football on gravel. It is immeasurably easier to play football in Iceland than it was 20 years ago. Like the lone dribbler in his snood in

Bodø, Icelandic children now have a space to emulate their heroes.

Besides, the idea of an Icelandic mentality runs deeper than artificial turf.

## Chapter Four
# Grit and sawdust

THE WORLD powerlifting champion barely remembers the moments that define his career.

Rúnar Geirmundsson laughs as I recoil from the cause of his amnesia. It is a small jar of ammonia, at once cleansing and corrosive. Tears form and my throat burns. As Rúnar returns the jar to a bench my blurry eyes are drawn to the tattoo on the back of his head – the contorted red face of the devil squints from behind a tight fade.

'Pretty strong, right?' he says, nodding to the ammonia. 'It increases your blood flow but also gives you this kind of blackout feeling. I don't remember most of my lifts in competition.'

We are in Thor's Power Gym, an austere industrial unit in Kópavogur. It is the place to explore the construct of a unique Icelandic mentality – the idea that Icelanders are somehow more driven or tougher than others.

The guttural croak of heavy metal rumbles through the air that smells rubbery and sweet. Rúnar uses a winch to roll two strips of thick cloth – like the ones boxers use to protect their hands – into taut coils. He unravels them around his knees, grappling and tightening as he wraps. Satisfied that his joints are secure, he totters to the bar. He rubs his hands along the metal, releasing a wispy cloud of chalk that settles on the black floor. Rúnar grunts through the final set of squats in his Wednesday workout. The vein on his left temple dilates as lactic acid rises in his thighs.

Hafþór Júlíus Björnsson is the owner of the gym. He gazes menacingly, arms crossed, from a poster on the wall. Box-set gorgers know him as Gregor 'The Mountain' Clegane from *Game of Thrones*, but acting is not his main focus. Hafþór won the 2018 World's Strongest Man competition and has finished on the podium every year since 2012. He is a colossus of tattooed granite held together by steel wire. Thor's Power Gym is where the giants train. And they train hard. Icelandic athletes have been crowned the World's Strongest Man nine times. Americans are the only nationality to have won more, with 12 titles.

Rúnar became the International Powerlifting League (IPL) world champion in Las Vegas in 2017. He also works as a photographer, manages a clothing label and is about to join an Australian deathcore band as guest vocalist on the European leg of their tour.

'That's the Icelandic way,' he says. 'We work way too much. That's how we're brought up. Your parents, grandparents, great-grandparents, all of them worked really hard because life was tough here, man. Really tough. That sticks in your genes.'

We talk in the kitchen, on leather sofas that lost their showroom sheen a long time ago. We are away from the tractor tyres and boulders in the gym but far from comfort.

That is not the purpose of this place. A tub ominously labelled 'Dark Matter' stands beside the Nescafe on the surface.

Rúnar's routine revolves around being stronger and better than the day before. He wakes up at the same time, always. He goes to sleep at the same time, always. Between training, eating, massages and physiotherapy, there is little time for frivolity.

'I'm turning 27 and I've been powerlifting competitively for 11 years. I have no social life, man. You won't see me downtown. You won't see me at parties. I've never tasted alcohol in my entire life. I don't know what beer tastes like. I don't know what cigarettes taste like. Whatever substance it is, I've never tried it because I've always been on a mission.

'People go to Ibiza after they graduate and shit like that. I've had no time for that. My social life is in the gym. I probably haven't experienced as much as other people my age, but I think I've done cooler stuff. I get to travel the world doing what I love. I want to build a legacy. When I'm dead I want people to know who I was, so I guess I'll have to sacrifice those little things.'

Rúnar has a phrase tattooed across his forehead, just behind the hairline. 'I'll rest when I'm dead.' He takes it literally.

'I just wanted to be something other than what I was: a little kid in the west. I grew up on the western peninsula, my parents ran a prison, and it's hard to get out of there, you know? I wanted to be something different. That's why I'm covered in tattoos. I want to be something different.'

He settled on powerlifting. 'You don't get any help from the government. No money. Nothing. It's all about you and what you do. I like going the hard way and thriving against all odds. I like that.'

Does this relentless pursuit of notoriety and fulfilment become lonely? 'I'm lucky enough to have a fiancée who supports everything I do. If I didn't have her it would be lonely because you do all of that and, when the day is done, you're lying in bed alone.'

Rúnar has endured a frustrating few months. An elbow injury has prevented him from training fully. Although he comfortably squats a barbell that droops on each side with the weight of the plates, inactivity has sapped his strength.

And the moment he became world champion – the achievement of his life – was anticlimactic. He explains in his itinerant mid-Atlantic accent:

'I always said that when I became world champion I would be happy, I would be finished, ecstatic. I was chasing that for 11 years, and actually it was kind of disappointing. My brother was with me. He was celebrating, fucking holding me and jumping around. I was like, "Yeah, yeah, yeah, this is good." But I didn't think it was good. It was the end goal, but it didn't finish how I wanted. I didn't get the numbers I wanted. It was bittersweet. More bitter than sweet, I think.'

The realisation dawned on Rúnar. What now? Was that it? All that graft for an underwhelming moment experienced through an ammonia-induced fog? He recalibrated and looked to the long term.

'I think one year ahead or five years ahead. That's the time span I think in. I don't think about next week or next month. I'm really patient.'

Like the other Icelanders with a penchant for pumping iron, Rúnar displays the mental qualities that Angela Lee Duckworth – professor of psychology at the University of Pennsylvania – identified in studies of successful Ivy League students, cadets at the West Point Military Academy and even Spelling Bee maestros. They all had grit, which she defines as 'passion and perseverance for very long-term goals'.

Duckworth elaborated in a TED talk: 'Grit is sticking with your future, day in, day out, not just for the week, not just for the month, but for years, and working hard to make that future a reality. Grit is living life like it's a marathon, not a sprint.'

Grit is intangible and thus difficult to quantify. Duckworth developed the 'grit scale' in an attempt to do just that. It is based on self-assessment questionnaires, which are prone to contaminate grit with ego. Nevertheless, Grétar Steinsson would score high. The former Bolton Wanderers full-back grew up in Siglufjörður, a low-rise fishing town on the melancholy north coast. He joined Fleetwood Town as sporting director in January 2015. Shirtsleeves now cover his tattoos but cannot conceal his cauldron intensity that lassoes you into listening.

It is Monday morning at Fleetwood's pristine training ground. The club sacked the head coach, Uwe Rösler, on Saturday evening. I expected the interview to be cancelled. Yet after ten minutes of pacing the on-site restaurant with iPhone to ear, Grétar talks for over an hour with little prompting.

He tells a story from his childhood. 'There was one guy from Siglufjörður who always wore shorts. All year round he wore shorts. He would take me mountain running. I was 14 or 15. My body wasn't developed to do this distance running. But he would take me out mountain running and I built this threshold for never stopping.'

Grétar applied that capacity for endurance to football. His friend's father managed the sports centre in the town. Grétar was always in there, always trusted to turn off the lights and pull the cover back over the swimming pool.

'I was very young when I said, "I'm going to be a professional footballer." That was the mentality I had. I would cut out interviews with players. I had a sticker of Eiður Guðjohnsen on the wall and loads of posters. I was just obsessed with football. Absolutely obsessed.

'I was very much about competing, winning, practising. I kept a diary every day. If I went swimming, I wrote how many lengths I did. I was absolutely obsessed with everything. I don't know how the people in the town saw me. Probably as a bit of an oddball with a raging temper.'

Grétar's parents accepted that their fiercely driven son was not for turning, so they prepared him for life as a footballer. 'I was very young when my family said, "Right, if you want to become a footballer you need to learn to live like one,"' Grétar recalls. He would have to move abroad to play professional football, so his family encouraged extra work on foreign languages. He now speaks English, German and Dutch. Young footballers live alone, so his family coerced him into cleaning and laundry. Footballers need good nutrition, so they taught him to balance carbs and protein. Grétar's mother did not allow him to leave Iceland before graduating from school. She taught her son to finish what he had started.

Grétar made his first move as a teenager. He crossed the country to ÍA Akranes, then the strongest club in Iceland. It was the right environment at the right point in his development.

'Akranes was probably the highest-performing town I've been in. The competition was fierce. I wasn't just competing against local boys, who were very good, but also against professionals, former professionals, top foreign players who had been brought in. Not winning was not an option in that town.

'I was fortunate in that the principal of the school was also part of the football club. I probably had the lowest attendance. If one of the local boys was in the gym, I would skip class and go to the gym. It was non-stop. You had to win. You had to perform at the highest level. That was where I developed, it was that grit of, "You've got to succeed," otherwise you'll get stamped on and kicked out.'

He was still in Akranes at 22. Still semi-professional. Injury and restlessness would have lured less gritty individuals to make irrational decisions. Grétar, by contrast, turned down foreign clubs because they did not fit his long-term goals.

'I declined a lot of clubs,' he says. 'Stoke City made an offer and I declined them because I didn't want to play in the Championship. Guðjón Þórðarson, who was the manager at the time, said, "Who the fuck do you think you are?"'

Stoke had Icelandic owners, an Icelandic coach and a strong Icelandic contingent in the squad. It would have been the easy move.

'I wasn't big-headed, but it didn't fit my plan. I always had a plan and a tick box of what I wanted to do. I never claimed I was the best, but Stoke didn't fit the plan. At the time I was very athletic, very fit, very mentally strong, but technically and tactically I wasn't very good. It was my belief that if I went to Europe, to Holland, and added those things to what I already had, I could play in the Premier League.'

And so it turned out. Grétar joined Young Boys in Switzerland and then AZ Alkmaar in the Netherlands. He worked on the weaknesses in his game and in 2008 progressed to the Premier League. Passion and perseverance for a very long-term goal.

Grétar's phone and notepad remain untouched on the table. He says something illuminating as, in the background, the Fleetwood squad trot out to begin their warm-up beneath the beady stare of three circling seagulls.

'We're a confident nation. We always believe we're going to win Eurovision before we enter it. And we're a growth-mindset nation. We just believe that we can succeed. We're a tiny island in the middle of the Atlantic Ocean with 333,000 people. But we still believe we can achieve anything.'

It is significant that Grétar identifies a growth mindset in Iceland. Carol Dweck, professor of psychology at Stanford University, coined the term after studying thousands of students in the United States. People with a growth mindset – as opposed to a fixed mindset – believe ability is not innate and that we can improve with effort. With the appropriate opportunities and support we can change how intelligent we are. People with a growth mindset view setbacks as a prompt to work harder, rather than confirmation that they are not good enough.

There is relatively little research on how grit is developed. But, as far as Angela Lee Duckworth can tell with the available information, establishing a growth mindset is the best way to create a gritty culture. Her research shows that, although there is no correlation between talent and grit, growth mindset and grit go hand in hand.

This is particularly clear in Iceland. While other countries reward ability or talent, Icelanders praise mettle. Football coaches often accompany staccato applause with a shout of *duglegur* when a young player has done well. Parents use the same word when their toddler takes its first steps or says its first words. Literally translated, it means something will 'suffice' – it is enough. But *duglegur* has come to encompass determination, hard work and bravery. In essence, it means grit.

Conscientious parents, teachers and coaches around the world devour literature that explains how to nurture a growth mindset in children. In Iceland, the traditional vocabulary does the job organically.

Another phrase cuts deep into the Icelandic psyche: þetta reddast. It is used to express faith that everything will work out well in the end. It was a coping mechanism when long, bitter winters whipped Iceland. People had to believe that problems would work themselves out and solutions would present themselves. That belief was all that kept insanity at the door.

Þetta reddast remains a prevalent attitude to life. A 2017 poll conducted by the University of Iceland revealed that 45 per cent of Icelanders live their life according to the saying. There is a strong belief in the idea that if the right effort is applied, things will fall into place. It is easier to accept setbacks with this attitude to life.

Grétar and Rúnar are salient examples of a common character type: gritty, driven, single-minded. Grétar sees his reflection in a lot of his fellow Icelanders. Iceland's past reveals why these characteristics have sunk into the nation's self-perception.

This is a passage from Guðrún Guðmundsdóttir's autobiography. She was born in 1860 as one of ten siblings, five of whom died in early childhood. Guðrún recalls the moment her eight-year-old brother died suddenly in bed while she was tending to their baby sister:

> I raced around the floor holding the baby and crying. I harped on the same sentence again and again: 'I want to die too. I want to die too.'
>
> 'Maybe you will,' answered my mother. That was all she said to comfort me. Next my father was fetched and Bergur, my little brother, was put into an appropriate position. I did not see my parents cry and I did not cry for long. Thereafter, my parents went to work in the vegetable garden and I was left with the baby and the corpse.

Her experience is representative of many that Sigurður Gylfi Magnússon, a social historian, encountered in a study of 240 autobiographies written by Icelanders born in the late 19th century.

The landscape was a malevolent force that teased its inhabitants. A lack of useful land meant each farm was isolated by necessity. Earthquakes and volcanic eruptions struck periodically, often resulting in famine and disease. The North Atlantic was perilous for those who scraped a living from the open deck of a fishing boat. Death was another part of life.

Guðrún's exposure to infant mortality was the norm rather than the exception. Children watched the most important people in their life die before their eyes. They were left alone, with scant emotional support, to process the grief. It is little wonder they sought refuge in the pages of a book, where the narrative provided an escape and the neat lines of text a semblance of order. But the reality was bleaker than the world described on paper.

Children worked on the farm from the age of five or six. This involved minding sheep, often at night and far from the dim lights of home.

Sigurður Jónsson, born in 1863, explained the exasperation:

> When I was nine years old I had to round up the sheep, which were milked every day, but they were difficult to deal with. They usually wandered well into the interior. In these areas I had many tears.
>
> When a sheep was missing, I was always sent out again in search, often into the night. Sometimes the search was unsuccessful and I could not find the sheep and it had totally vanished. My father, who was very insensitive, once sent me out in the dark and thick fog, while the others went to sleep.

> I started to walk and cried and threw myself down
> a short distance from the farm.

Sigurður's mother sent a farmhand out to fetch him.

Meanwhile, popular tales about trolls, elves and other creatures that went bump in the night were all regaled while the family worked the wool. Such stories intensified the torment. Children were conditioned to fear the dark nights and all that they hid, but the darkness was exactly where they were sent.

The environment broke some children but others thrived. Many of the peasants in Sigurður Gylfi Magnússon's study reflected fondly on their formative years and emerged with a psyche shaped by the Sagas – a belief that they could take on the world and anything it might throw at them. Icelanders who grew up playing football on gravel pitches, in all weather, often have a similar attitude. They see their youth as arduous yet necessary to chisel grit into their character.

Although Guðrún and Sigurður were born in the 1860s, life for most Icelandic people did not significantly change for another century.

Arni Helgason, born in 1914, blamed strenuous work for the two-year bout of polio he suffered from the age of ten:

> I was only six or seven years old when I started
> helping in the baiting shed, baiting fish lines. It was
> cold and hard work. I am convinced – though it
> has never been proven – that it was working in the
> baiting shed that did it for me. As a boy I worked for

hours on end baiting the lines and stacking the tubs.
It was a heavy load for a young child to have to bear.

It is not too crude an oversimplification to say the Second
World War provoked a period of rapid change in Iceland, as
the economy benefited from Allied occupation and Marshall
Aid. Up to that point, everyday life remained the same for
many Icelanders. Housing and sanitation remained poor,
for example. Over 50 per cent of houses were made of turf
in 1910, and that figure still hovered at 11 per cent in 1940.

What does this have to do with football? More than
it may appear.

Footballers do not exist in a vacuum. Where their
parents and grandparents come from matters, because we
are products of the society we are part of. The values of our
culture and the people around us have a profound effect
on who we are. The grandparents and great-grandparents
of current footballers grew up in extremely primitive
conditions, with stoicism and industriousness placed on
a pedestal.

Those values remain relatively undiluted in contemporary Icelandic society. Hard work is venerated.
Teenagers spend a large chunk of their summer holidays
working on council-sponsored employment schemes –
planting flowers or picking litter from verges. Many of
their parents work more than one job. Irina Sazonova, the
Russia-born gymnast who represented Iceland at the 2016
Olympics, held down three jobs while she prepared for the
tournament: coaching in a local gym, delivering pizzas and
cleaning hotel rooms.

Footballers embrace the values that sustained Iceland for centuries.

Matthías Vilhjálmsson spent his youth in Ísafjörður, in the extreme north-west of Iceland. In the winter he practised overhead kicks with the cushion of a two-metre layer of snow. In summer a farmer let the local boys play in a field among grazing sheep. Now Matthías plays for Vålerenga after several seasons at Rosenborg, the dominant force in Norwegian football.

'We think we're quite tough,' he admits. 'There's a "never give up" attitude, no matter what happens. That's our culture. The life we live.

'The quality of life is much better now than in the early days, but we still have these real working-class people. My father still lives in Ísafjörður. He's worked on a shrimp farm for 20 or 30 years. Before that, he worked in fishing. He leaves at 6.30 in the morning, comes home at 4.30, and never complains. So if I were to complain about having two sessions in one day, he would slap me, for sure!'

Quality of life has certainly improved in Iceland. By almost any measure, from social mobility to happiness to poverty levels, Iceland ranks as one of the most affluent and equal societies in the world. Yet this does not validate the myth that Iceland is classless. Sarah Moss – a British academic and writer – worked for a year at the University of Iceland in the aftermath of the financial crisis. In *Names for the Sea* Moss reflects on a perception among Icelanders that inequality is something that happens elsewhere. Some students told her that there was no class system, but perhaps this alienation from poverty proves Icelandic social inequality. The chasm between middle class and poor is so great that the existence of the poor is news to the middle class. While it is true that Moss's time in Iceland coincided with a period of acute financial strife, when food bank use and other markers of social inequality were starker than usual, her observations remain important. Iceland is a good place to live but not a classless utopia.

Because of its relative affluence, however, Iceland is not a natural setting for the accepted rags-to-riches narrative of the footballer. Diego Maradona, Pelé, and countless others relied on talent to claw themselves out of poverty and provide for their families in fiercely unequal societies. There is a sense that this arduous path creates a single-mindedness and determination that players from more comfortable backgrounds do not possess. Though there may be an element of truth to this theory, it is romanticised. Most footballers succeed despite poverty, not because of it. A budding teenager cannot flourish if there is no food on the table, nobody to lean on for a lift to training, or if he is working long hours to supplement the family income.

The vast majority of Icelanders are in a privileged position in that football is not a route out of poverty. Iceland is a wealthy social democracy that encourages all citizens to play sport and provides the infrastructure to do so. Yet this supportive background does not mean that Icelandic players lack desire. They draw it from elsewhere; from the harsh conditions, the entrenched values of hard work, and the knowledge that emigration is a necessary sacrifice in the pursuit of professional football.

Aron Gunnarsson, the Iceland captain, discussed motivation in a 2018 interview with the *Reykjavík Grapevine*.

Generation after generation, we've had to stick together to survive in harsh conditions. Darkness, wind and freezing cold. That breeds togetherness and willingness to stand up for each other when it really counts. I'm proud of those roots. I'm proud to belong to a country built by hard workers who did what they needed to do to survive. Whenever I pull on the national team shirt it reminds me to appreciate where I'm from and be grateful to those who were before me.

This idea that shared struggle breeds collective determination is not unique to Iceland. Luka Modrić – the Croatia and Real Madrid midfielder – explained the adhesive effects of the Balkan War in a 2011 interview with the *Daily Mail*.

'You have to understand something about the Croatian people. After everything that has happened, after the war, we are stronger, tougher. What we've been through was not easy. The war made us stronger. We are not easy people to break. It's hard to break us and there is a determination to show that. To show that we can succeed.'

Iceland and Croatia both manage to compete with far bigger nations. Perhaps there is something in the self-perception of hereditary mental strength.

'Measuring mental toughness is the holy grail,' says Daði Rafnsson, who is in pursuit of that elusive knowledge. Daði is the former head of youth at Breiðablik and a respected voice in the coaching community. Following a spell coaching in China, he is researching mental strength in sport for a PhD. He believes that hard work runs through Icelandic society as a golden thread, but acknowledges that in football the woolly notion of 'guts' is vulnerable to romanticisation.

'Mental toughness is something that we supposedly have plenty of,' he says in a soft baritone voice. 'Every country makes its own myths and expectations. When the Iceland women's team played Brazil here, you heard some of the players and coaches saying, "We're better fighters than them. Our mentality is so strong."

'I've coached Brazilian national team players. They have an incredible mentality. Professional to the core. Incredibly tough. They could withstand many conditions that Icelanders could not. So what is this toughness we're talking about?'

It is generally risky to ascribe national characteristics to a population. In the case of Iceland, however, it is less crude. The population is small and far more homogenous than Brazil, for example, where there are stark racial and social inequalities.

With that in mind, it is fair to suggest that Icelandic footballers would rank high on the grit scale. They have to be gritty. Facilities have improved, but artificial turf does not keep out the wind and rain. They must leave their friends and family behind in pursuit of professional football. They need an intrinsic motivation that others do not. That is not to say that Icelandic teams work harder on the pitch than their foreign opponents; rather that Icelandic youngsters grow up in a culture that equips them with the mental tools to make the most of their talent.

Siggi Eyjólfsson, the former technical director of the KSÍ, opened his eyes to this when he went to coach at Lillestrøm in Norway. Siggi divides footballers into three groups:

- Player One plays football because it is fun. He likes to be with his friends, but attendance at training is sketchy and he is not ambitious to improve.
- Player Two wants to be better. He wants to improve and is willing to do extra training to achieve that.
- Player Three wants to be the best. He structures his life around football. The coach has to drag him off the training pitch and force him to rest.

Siggi has coached in Norway and China. He played in the United States, Belgium and England. He thinks that Player Two and Player Three are more common in Iceland than in those countries. There are a lot of gritty kids with the perseverance and passion to pursue the dream of playing professionally and representing Iceland.

More research in this direction is necessary. Haukur Ingi Guðnason moved into psychology after a professional career that included a brief spell at Liverpool in the late 1990s. In 2006, Haukur Ingi asked 116 Icelandic footballers to complete a self-assessment questionnaire. The results were unsurprising. The respondents who had played for Iceland at senior level had better mental skills than those who only played for Iceland at youth level.

Research comparing Icelandic and non-Icelandic youngsters on the grit scale would be useful. Until research offers evidence to the contrary, my hunch is that a unique Icelandic mentality is a myth. Icelanders are just gritty. Footballers are two or three branches down the family tree from people who faced a struggle to survive in a primitive environment that dislocates the senses. Industriousness was, and remains, a core value. This culture cultivates grit. That, in turn, helps explain why Iceland produces a disproportionate number of professional footballers, weightlifters and musicians.

There is also another layer to the question of mentality. If Icelandic players firmly believe that they are mentally tougher than their opponents, does the reality matter? Icelanders are under the influence of a performance-enhancing placebo effect.

Diego Johannesson – known to all as Diegui – grew up on Spain's ragged north coast. He is one of triplets born to a Spanish mother and an Icelandic father. Diegui plays for Real Oviedo in the Spanish Segunda División and made his Iceland debut in 2016.

In a cafe in an upmarket *barrio* of Oviedo, I ask Diegui if he believes in a specific Icelandic mentality. He pauses for a moment. 'Clearly the population is small,' he responds. 'But it's the Icelandic blood, it's the Viking blood and I never give up on anything.'

He maintains eye contact. 'I give all I have. If there's a ball heading out of play and it's clear that I won't make it in time, I'll try and stop it anyway. I think that is the basis of the success Iceland is experiencing right now.'

Icelandic exceptionalism is often framed as 'Viking spirit', which Aron Gunnarsson defines as 'the spirit of Nordic people giving their all to survive in hard conditions'. It is about projecting an image of strength and virility to the world. Gunnarsson, with his shrubby beard and Old Norse tattoos across his chest and back, fuels this projection. Icelandic footballers are presented as modern-day Vikings – heroic ambassadors of the nation who use effective tactics to triumph against stronger opposition. They are not, however, the first group of young Icelandic men to have metaphorical horned helmets thrust on their heads. In a 2005 speech in London, Ólafur Ragnar Grímsson, then the president of Iceland, trumpeted the virtues of 'young entrepreneurial Vikings', the raucous financiers invading foreign markets. This rhetoric was pompous, vacuous and hubristic; the holy trinity of doomed political discourse.

There is no evidence that 'Viking spirit' brings any physiological or mental benefits. Players from Reykjavík and Rome and Riyadh will run just as hard. But in the stifling intensity of a match, as the clock ticks past 90 minutes, if a player believes he can draw extra energy because of Viking blood, the veracity is unimportant. The player has gained an advantage regardless.

The placebo effect can reach the opposition, too. Tim Sparv captained Finland to a narrow victory over Iceland in 2017. Over the phone from Denmark, where he holds the midfield for FC Midtjylland, he explains his perception of the Iceland team.

'They all work for each other. It's a real team effort. They might have one or two stars in their team but even they are really humble, hard-working. I think somebody who symbolises that would be their captain with the long beard. I mean, that's how I see Icelandic people: strong, bearded, working hard and being very humble in what they do.'

If Icelandic players believe they are mentally stronger than others, and opponents also associate them with endurance and durability, it becomes a self-fulfilling prophecy. Icelanders think of themselves as people who can overcome adversity, which often leads to behaviour that fits this self-perception. Young players want to conform. It proliferates.

On an island where grit and a growth mindset have sunk into the rocks and stayed, the five words etched into Rúnar Geirmundsson's scalp – 'I'll rest when I'm dead' – are more doctrine than decoration.

Fishermen have a more acute understanding of this than most.

# Chapter Five
# Iceland v Nigeria

NEON BLUE lights lend the narrow staircase the hue of a nightclub corridor. Biggi Sverrisson sits on his throne at the top. Cigarette smoke floats from his pale lips and forms a bluish haze in the wheelhouse. We are on *Vestmannaey*, a 29-metre trawler built in Gdansk in 2007, and my home for five days.

Biggi is the captain. Fourteen screens blink information at him from a concave booth. I had imagined panels of varnished teak and ornate compasses, but the wheelhouse bears a closer resemblance to a space shuttle. There is no knobbly, nautical steering wheel. A doorknob-sized dial, positioned beside an ashtray and two cupholders, controls the course of the boat.

I grasp the surfaces to keep my balance and try to avoid touching anything on the various control panels. There are discarded vape machines strewn across the surfaces. I presume they belong to the first mate. Captain Biggi does not seem the vaping type. Right on cue, he taps a second cigarette from a fresh pack of Winston's and lights it with a Zippo. The lighter is decorated with the image of a golden Labrador puppy snuggling with a black kitten.

'We'll steam to the east for a couple of hours,' he grunts. His voice is coarse and deep. Plosive syllables sound like the croak of a bullfrog. A souvenir Euro 2016 T-shirt clings to his paunch. Before coming aboard I asked if I needed to bring food. 'No, no,' Biggi replied with a pat of his belly, 'we have a good chef and we eat well.'

Biggi is a football obsessive, as are most of his crew. He delayed our departure until nine o'clock in the evening because he wanted to watch Argentina play Croatia in a private bar he co-owns with four fellow fishermen. He supports Manchester United, but a bundle of Liverpool bedding awaited me in my cabin. It looked like it was from the early 2000s. It took me back to 12 May 2001 and a kick-about at my friend Will's house. That afternoon, Michael Owen scored two late goals for Liverpool to beat Arsenal in the FA Cup Final. After the final whistle, with the garage door for a goal, we took turns to be Owen.

Biggi knows these waters well. He first went to sea at 15. At 19 he 'went to the wheelhouse' as the captain's mate. By 25 he was a captain himself. Even in a culture where men go to sea when they are still boys, Biggi was unusually precocious. Now in his mid-fifties, he has been at sea for 40 years.

It runs in the blood. 'My father was the captain on a cargo vessel,' he says. 'In the old days they sailed from Iceland to Spain and then on to the Philippines or somewhere like that. They were travelling all around the world. In the old days, when I was born, he was away for six or seven months at a time.' Biggi used to go to sea for six-week voyages on a larger boat with a crew of 26. But the trips were too long and family too distant. *Vestmannaey* goes to sea for three to five days.

We are waiting for the haddock to come. Biggi knows that when the herring go down to the depths of the ocean to lay their larvae, the haddock will feed on it and grow. 'About a week,' he mutters, 'in a week they will come.' *Vestmannaey* has the biggest haddock quota in Iceland and that quota will rise by 40 per cent next year in tandem with fish stocks. It is the dollar-ringed catch for Biggi and his crew.

'Fishing is mostly experience,' he says. 'It is mainly just my sense that I use to fish. We've been there, we know it, we write it down. It's very easy for me to go out and fish these days because I've been doing it for such a long time. Sometimes there is nothing. You can't panic. You can never panic.'

That reliance on instinct seems incongruous with the wall of screens in front of him. But they are just an aid. There is no substitute for the fisherman's intuition. Before GPS and sonar, fishermen lowered a length of string over the side of the boat to measure the depth. They used another device to scrape a sample of the ocean floor so the captain knew the surface below. New technology advances relentlessly. *Vestmannaey* is only 11 years old, yet Biggi has a new boat under construction in Norway.

'At the moment I can only see what is beneath my boat. Now they have these drones that the captain controls with a joystick, so he can look for fish over there or over there.' He gestures loosely to either side of the boat and pauses. 'Maybe that will take the fun out of it.'

I totter across the wheelhouse to the back window with the grace of a newborn giraffe. The sea is rough. Flecks of white appear and disappear on the crests of the waves. I feel behind my right ear for the circular plaster I bought earlier that afternoon. Seasickness prevention for three days, apparently. I gulp down the rising bloat in my stomach and distract myself. A computer shows the weather forecast on a desk tucked in the back corner. My eyes are drawn to the pop-up advertisements that appear based on search history. All of them promise 'the lowest prices' for flights from Reykjavík to Moscow.

'Do you still feel excited when you leave the harbour?' I ask.

'Yes, yes, yes,' Biggi says. 'You are always trying to be the best boat. We were on top in Iceland but then we went to the dry dock for two weeks. There are two boats trying to get above us, but we will take them later on.'

A muffled message wafts through the radio. Biggi barks a quick reply. 'That was my friend in another boat,' he explains. 'We are just talking about where we are going to look for the fish. We want to be the best. But we never lie to each other. We tell each other what is going on.' Biggi extinguishes his second cigarette and reaches for the phone. 'Time to shoot the net,' he says with gusto.

One minute passes before Óli, the chief engineer, comes upstairs to operate the winches. He raises his eyebrows in my direction. 'How are you doing?' he asks.

Biggi answers on my behalf. 'Matt is good. He has sailor's blood.' I beam inwardly, as if avoiding seasickness is some kind of affirmation of masculinity.

Óli takes control of the joysticks on a panel at the back of the wheelhouse. The winch crunches and begins to gyrate. Biggi leans against the window and holds a radio up to his mouth. He relays instructions to the helmeted men on deck, who are linked to the wheelhouse by earpieces. There is a problem. The net is twisted.

'This never usually happens,' Biggi says before muttering something about the previous crew.

The deckhands wrestle with the net. They lean alarmingly close to the back of the boat, where the grey water swirls ominously. The grapple continues for ten minutes as Biggi broods in the window. Then out goes the net, 300 metres behind the boat, down to the sandbank where Biggi thinks the lemon sole will gather at this time in the evening. The boat stabilises, fixed to its course by the weight of the trawl. Óli jolts down the stairs and Biggi returns to his leather chair, content. The burble of the engine fills the silence.

I imagine how lonely it could be in the wheelhouse. Everything beyond the window feels malevolent when clouds descend and veering seagulls are the only sign of life. Icelanders used to fish from open rowing boats, in an age when families spent long winters huddled around the flicker of an open flame, absorbing folklore tales of mysterious creatures at sea. Most were, understandably, cautionary tales. One such yarn told of a whale monster known as *Lyngbakr* that protruded from the surface disguised as an island covered with a mauve carpet of heather. It served as a reminder to give unfamiliar islands a wide berth.

In Biggi's wheelhouse, the Wi-Fi, television and satellite phone hold nature – and its mystical creatures – at bay.

Yet it must be a lonely place when impenetrable darkness descends. Biggi sighs. 'The hardest part is when there are no fish. Especially if it's bad weather. But you have the TV and we always find something. You always have to think.'

In that moment he reminded me of Santiago, the aged fisherman in Ernest Hemingway's *The Old Man and the Sea*. Santiago is dragged away from the Cuban coast by a giant marlin that has bitten his line. Santiago is weary but does not let go. He makes a vow: 'Fish, I'll stay with you until I'm dead.'

The contemporary captain bears a significant burden. The solitude is not literal. It does not come from being alone in the wheelhouse as the storm closes in. It takes the form of responsibility. If the captain fails to find fish, the crew return to shore with nothing. The deckhand tells his wife that they will struggle with the next mortgage payment. The chef wonders if he can pay the fees for his daughter to go on her football tour. That responsibility is the loneliness that weighs on the captain.

The sound of Simmi the chef singing Bob Marley's 'Three Little Birds' wafts through from the kitchen as Iceland v Nigeria draws closer.

He emerges with a bowl of nachos in one hand and a plate of sliced watermelon in the other. He grins manically, like Paul Gascoigne after he declared he was away to get his suit measured after the 1991 FA Cup semi-final. 'Waiting for the World Cup since 1947,' reads the message on his blue T-shirt.

Iceland has closed for the match. The banks shut at two o'clock for a three o'clock kick-off. The labour situation on *Vestmannaey* is the same. There will be no fishing this afternoon.

A crew member called Kristján emerges in a faded crimson T-shirt and skinny jeans from the stairs that lead down to the cabins. Like the rest of the crew, he walks on his toes. They are used to balancing. He dips his hand into a holdall and pulls out an oversized Iceland shirt. With blonde hair down to his shoulders, he would look more at home on Bondi Beach than on the deck of a trawler. But Kristján and fishing have an intertwined history. A photo of his grandfather overlooks Biggi's throne in the wheelhouse: a former captain who now hangs as a guiding presence.

Kristján's immediate family is equally distinguished. His father, Birkir Kristinsson, played 74 matches as a goalkeeper for the Iceland national team between 1988 and 2004. Kristján's uncle, meanwhile, was a board member at Stoke City when the club was under Icelandic ownership. Kristján may have followed his grandfather to sea, but he has a rich heritage in football.

The rest of the crew file in and pull nylon goodies from the holdall. They squeeze into the booths and try to eat the watermelon without the juices dropping on to their shirts.

Finnur sits opposite me. He chuckles and angles his phone to show me a series of Snapchat videos from his friends in Volgograd. Upstairs, Biggi has switched the biggest of his screens to the football and set the boat to autopilot.

The crew are tense. Finnur claps and rubs his hands as if nervousness will escape through his palms. He strains to reach a bag of *Harðfiskur* – a fish jerky made by drying unsalted cod on wooden racks – from the table. The English poet W.H. Auden spent three months in Iceland in 1936 and was overexposed to *Harðfiskur*. 'The tougher kind tastes like toenails,' he concluded, 'and the softer kind tastes like the skin off the soles of one's feet.' At least it is chewy enough to burn some vapours of nervous energy.

The teams come out. The anthem begins. The crew mumble the words. Kick-off brings silence but for the hum of the engine and the clink of the condiment bottles huddling in a basket next to the TV. By the time the Viking clap indicates that 12 minutes have passed, Iceland are on top. Gylfi Sigurðsson has twice sent shots through the smothering 32°C heat and into the arms of Francis Uzoho, Nigeria's teenage goalkeeper.

Simmi the chef nervously works away at his incisors with a toothpick. Valtýr runs a hand through his ginger hair, which distorts the shape of the star tattooed around his elbow. Five of the crew are huddled together in the central booth. I sense their proximity is partly for the view of the TV and partly because the contact reminds them there is a world beyond the all-consuming green on the screen.

The floating observers lean forwards in unison as Alfreð Finnbogason glances an inviting free kick wide of the post. The half-time whistle follows shortly after. Iceland are in control. As the Icelanders amble down the tunnel to escape the heat, Gernot Rohr, Nigeria's German coach, addresses his players on the pitch.

The door to the wheelhouse swings open and Biggi emerges to refill his mug with coffee. 'Pretty good,' he grunts before returning upstairs with a slice of watermelon. He will fly back out to Russia if Iceland reach the last 16.

Whatever Rohr said on the pitch had an effect. Four minutes into the second half, Nigeria clear one of Aron Gunnarsson's catapult throw-ins and gallop forwards on the counter-attack. Ahmed Musa, the waspish forward, fizzes into the Iceland box and reaches the ball before a dozy Ragnar Sigurðsson. He cushions it with a silken touch and fires beyond Hannes Halldórsson. Silence. Chastened silence as everyone tries to work out how Iceland conceded a goal from a position of such strength. Iceland do the counter-attacks; they don't get counter-attacked.

Nigeria begin to suffocate Iceland. Blackness fills the screen for a fleeting moment as the 'bad or no signal' message appears. It is more of a relief than a frustration. The curtains sway with the tide.

Nigeria, and Musa, punish Iceland's lethargy with a second goal. He leaves Kári Árnason in his wake, shimmies past Hannes and rolls the ball into the empty net. His bombast and pace are too much.

Five minutes pass. The crew snap out of their dejection with a yell. Alfreð Finnbogason flicks the ball with his toe deep inside the box and falls under the lead-footed challenge of Tyronne Ebuehi. The referee dismisses the claim, but then pauses and puts a finger to his ear to amplify the message from the VAR lair. We agonise and search for meaning in his furrowed brow. His finger drops back down and he draws a box in the air to indicate that he's going to have another look. The slow-motion replays show a clear foul. He gives the penalty.

Valgeir stands in the semi-darkness of the mess with his hands clasped behind his head. Gylfi places the ball deliberately, straightens his back and exhales.

'NEEEEEEEY.'

There is a guttural release as Gylfi scoops the ball over the crossbar and into the crowd. I puff my cheeks in exasperation and hope for his sake that the miss does not become important for goal difference in the group's final standings. The whistle ends a meek second half. Nigeria could not muster a shot before the break; after the interval they had 16.

The crew allow themselves five minutes of mourning before the shirts go back in the holdall. There are fish to catch.

It is 48 hours since Iceland's defeat to Nigeria. Four of the crew are slouched across the blue vinyl seating in the mess. It is bright outside but the curtains are pegged to the wall. The glow from yet another Netflix series illuminates their jaded faces.

I am still wearing my England shirt after watching Harry Kane score a hat-trick in the midday kick-off against porous Panama. Biggi had insisted that they switched the TV from Icelandic coverage of the match to the BBC. And, as it is Sunday, a full English breakfast was on the menu. Simmi the chef had sauntered through from the kitchen wearing a Greek-statue apron complete with chiselled torso and pert penis. He carried a plate piled with fried eggs, bacon, beans and toast. There I was, on an Icelandic trawler, having a more authentic experience of an England match than if I had watched in central London.

Ellert sits in the booth closest to the staircase down to the cabins and the bowels of the boat. He always sits in that seat, with his back to the wall and his slippers protruding into the gangway. Ellert pushes his headphones to the back of his head. They push his ears forwards. He turned 30 recently. It's his fourth year at sea. Before that he worked in a fishmeal factory back on the island. He was well dressed when he came aboard three days ago, with a beige parka jacket above black jeans and a pair of Doc Martens. A grey tracksuit has replaced the parka and his hair is unkempt.

'I've been with my girlfriend for 16 years and we have a baby son,' he tells me. A signed Iceland under-21 shirt hangs on the wall behind his left shoulder. A nudey calendar occupies the perpendicular wall in Ellert's alcove of choice. The calendar swings outwards with the movement of the boat in such a way that it looks like the scantily clad model is leering at the loopy signatures on the shirt.

'What did your girlfriend think when you decided to go to sea?' I ask.

'She was pretty pissed. But her father was a captain. Her grandfather was a captain. She knows what this lifestyle is like.'

The lifestyle Ellert refers to is a trade-off: a generous salary in exchange for a lot of time at sea. Most men go to sea at a young age, when the allure of money in the pocket is strong. The deckhands are at the bottom of the salary scale. They still earn the equivalent of a very comfortable six-figure salary in the United Kingdom. For Ellert, it was necessary to reach the first rung of the property ladder.

The abnormal work pattern – often two weeks on followed by one week off – suits a young, single fisherman. But his priorities change when he settles down with a partner. Home becomes harder to leave behind when the fisherman knows he will miss his child's birthday party.

The sea no longer represents the alloy wheels, the designer clothes and the reputation for always buying a round in the bar. The sea represents that nagging feeling that you wish you were somewhere else.

The seat squeaks as Ellert shuffles into a more comfortable position. 'On my first boat, the chief engineer was 68 and he had been at sea since he was 15. I'm not planning on staying for that long.'

Valgeir glances up from his MacBook. 'I tried to quit ten times,' he chirps.

'What stopped you?'

'The money. Once you have it, you get used to it, your girlfriend gets used to it, it's hard to give it up.'

The engine fills the silence again. Ellert changes the subject. 'You're here at the quietest time,' he says. 'June is dead. But between February and May it's insane. Sixteen hours of solid work every day. You have to get used to it, but you have to get used to this too.' He gestures to the inactivity. The crew lurch from intense manual labour to forced relaxation, concentration to boredom. The sedate atmosphere in the mess is laced with frustration. The fisherman's mentality is 'the more we catch, the sooner I can get home'. And, as they are paid according to the value of the catch, less fish means less money.

At least the risk is lower than it once was. 'All our safety equipment is brand new,' Ellert explains. 'We have these new lifejackets. When they're activated they send a signal to every boat within 100 miles. We have helmets, earpieces ... Those shows like *Deadliest Catch* are sensationalised. None of the crew have the safety equipment because it makes good TV when something goes wrong.'

We both look up to see kick-off in the match between Japan and Senegal. The match is barely ten seconds old when the phone from the wheelhouse rings. Ellert and Valgeir stand up and stretch in unison, each emitting a contorted grunt. They trudge past the kitchen and out to the stretch of corridor where their bibs and braces hang on individually named pegs, like the coats outside a classroom.

Once they have guided the net out to sea, they will return to the mess and wait until it fills. It could take 20 minutes. It could take three hours. Then they go back out to bring in the catch. The net slaps down on the red metal of the deck, dripping seawater and stray starfish. The fish go down a chute at the rear of the boat and on to a conveyor belt that rolls into the processing room. In there, the crew stand in single file, each with a chopping board in front of them and the conveyor belt to the left. The chef helps out. So do the engineers. It is all hands below deck. The metallic surfaces are spotless but the stench of fish guts still hangs in the air like a salty mist. Some of the fish on the belt flap pathetically. Once plucked by a gloved hand, it will be gutted and on the way to the cleaning machine and an icebox within five seconds.

I watch Japan v Senegal. I have become fond of my confined existence on *Vestmannaey*. My diet consists of three World Cup matches and Simmi's cooking. He worked as a baker before going to sea ten years ago and still makes a fine crusty loaf. Life is simple when the world measures 29 metres by ten.

Yet guilt gnaws at me because I am relaxing while the others work. I know I am being irrational. I have neither the gear nor the idea to contribute. But set against the irregular rhythm of the fisherman's life, a feeling of faint uselessness grows.

I enjoy going to the wheelhouse. Biggi ponders his next move while I lean over the side of his control panel, trying and failing to make sense of the smudge of colours that show what is entering the net. The weather is clear and the sea flat. The sun reflects off the Vatnajökull glacier, bright white against the light-blue sky. I have to squint to admire.

I ask Biggi about someone I suspect he will know. The man in question is also a fisherman in his mid-fifties, but he is known across the world for a feat of human endurance that prodded at the boundaries of science and wisdom.

'Guðlaugur Friðþórsson? Yes, I went to school with him,' Biggi says. He lights a cigarette and the sun refracts through the wispy plume of smoke. 'He's a great guy, a huge guy. He still lives on the island.'

Guðlaugur and Biggi were both young men looking to make a name for themselves at sea. And Biggi is right about his size. Guðlaugur was huge back then as well. He was a man-mountain – 1.93m tall and 125kg (6ft 4in and almost 20 stone) – with cherubic face and mousy hair that frizzed in tight curls.

Guðlaugur was one of a crew of five that left Vestmannaeyjar – a volcanic archipelago that dangles off the south coast of Iceland – on the morning of 11 March 1984. He was 23 at the time. Their vessel was called *Hellisey*. It was a trawler, but a small one by contemporary standards. The weather was good that day and the captain, 25-year-old Hjörtur Jónsson, chose to shoot the net six kilometres south-east of the island. It was a trip like any other. But things began to unravel at ten o'clock that evening.

'They were towing the trawl and it got stuck to something on the bottom,' Biggi rumbles as the cigarette gently billows in his right hand. 'When that happens you stop and you try to make it loose. But they didn't. I think something was wrong with the winch, so instead of pulling the trawl in, it pulled the boat over.'

Guðlaugur was below deck. He emerged as *Hellisey* capsized. Along with Hjörtur, the captain, and 21-year-old Pétur Sigurðsson, Guðlaugur scrambled on to the upturned bow. They tried to reach the lifeboat but it did not have an automatic release device. So they sat on the bow and they prayed. They prayed that they would reach shore together. Two of the crew had already died. Valur Smári Geirsson and Engilbert Eiðsson could not escape their cabins and drowned inside the upturned boat.

Guðlaugur and his two shivering companions knew that the *Hellisey* would soon sink to the seabed. The temperature of the sea was 5°C and the air above was a bitter -2°C. Flickers of yellow from the lighthouse at Stórhöfði, six kilometres away, lit the way to land. The three fishermen began to swim. They called each other's names, but after ten minutes Guðlaugur stopped hearing replies. He was alone.

He kept swimming. Stroke after stroke. He talked to the inquisitive birds that flew overhead. He talked to God. He thought about how he must stay alive to pay the final instalments on his motorbike. He kept a clear head throughout. He kept swimming.

About two hours had passed when a boat crossed within 100 metres of Guðlaugur. He yelled and flapped in a desperate attempt to get its attention. The boat continued on its course. The captain would not have heard him above the rattle of the engine and would not have seen him amid the darkness and swell. Guðlaugur kept swimming.

He kept swimming and three hours later Guðlaugur frothed against the black rocks of Heimaey's jagged east coast. He was on dry land, but the hope was false. The relentless waves and impassable cliffs meant he could not get out of the water. If he stayed too long, he would have been buffeted against the rocks. So he turned around, swam back out to sea and approached from a different angle.

The second attempt was a success. His ordeal, however, would continue. The nearest house was still two kilometres away and to reach it Guðlaugur had to cross a lava field in bare feet. He began to crawl, then tried to walk, then crawled again. He was aware that he could not stop to rest. If he slumped against a boulder and allowed sleep to engulf him, he would never wake up. Once he left the lava field behind, the weary fisherman passed a disused bathtub. It acted as a trough for grazing livestock. He punched through the layer of ice on the surface and lapped at the fresh water beneath.

It was just before seven o'clock when Guðlaugur summoned the dregs of his energy to bang on the door of Suðurgerður 2. Nearly nine hours had passed since *Hellisey* had capsized. Seventeen-year-old Freyr Atlason answered the door. He initially thought the man slumped in the porch was drunk. Then he noticed the puffy face, the sodden clothes and the mangled feet. Freyr fetched his father, Atli

Elíasson, who helped Guðlaugur to a chair and tucked him under a blanket. 'Swam, swam,' he muttered.

Atli later told *Morgunblaðið* that Guðlaugur had left a trail of bloodied footsteps on the pavement.

An ambulance arrived to whisk Guðlaugur to hospital. When the doctors took his temperature, it was too low to register on the thermometer. Simultaneously, coastguards powered out to sea to search for a trace of *Hellisey* and the four other fishermen. They found nothing. Guðlaugur was the only survivor. And not only that, he was discharged from hospital with no symptoms of hypothermia, just dehydration.

So how did Guðlaugur Friðþórsson survive? A normal human would have died after 30 minutes in such conditions. His feat of endurance aroused the curiosity of William Keatinge, a distinguished physiologist based in London. So, in an English hospital 17 months later, Guðlaugur re-enacted the night he cheated death. He wanted to contribute to research that may help fellow fishermen in similar situations. Keatinge watched as Guðlaugur lowered himself into a pool of cutting cold water at the same temperature as the sea off the Icelandic coast. The prim physiologist instructed him to move his arms and legs as if he were swimming. He kept moving. And kept moving. Keatinge had never seen anyone last for more than 30 minutes. Around 75 minutes into the trial, Guðlaugur asked to leave the pool. Not due to hypothermia, but because his feet hurt.

'Guðlaugur Friðþórsson is the only person to have survived such exceptional exposure to cold and be investigated afterwards,' Keatinge wrote in the *British*

*Medical Journal.* He concluded that Guðlaugur survived because his body was insulated by 14 millimetres of fat, almost twice the normal thickness. Or, as *New Scientist* less kindly put it, 'it is impossible not to be reminded of a seal and its sheath of blubber'.

Biggi does not remember Guðlaugur the death-defying phenomenon. He remembers the ruddy youngster scarred by the loss of four close friends.

'He went back to sea for a couple of years but he didn't like it,' Biggi says, 'and I don't think he wanted the attention from the film.'

The film Biggi refers to is *Djúpið* (*The Deep*), a 2012 release directed by Baltasar Kormákur. The film dramatised Guðlaugur's story well enough to earn an Oscar nomination in the foreign-language category.

'I see it as a reflection of who we are,' Iceland-born Kormákur told the *Reykjavík Grapevine.* 'American heroes wear capes, Icelandic heroes wear sea gear. This is the first time in Icelandic film history that someone deals with a tragedy at sea. This is the biggest scar we bear as a nation. Everyone knows someone who has lost someone at sea in Iceland. This is something that stands close to us. And we have never dealt with this.'

The problem, as far as I can glean from Biggi, was that Guðlaugur didn't see himself as an Icelandic hero. He was a young man troubled by the gnawing darkness of survivor's guilt.

After five days at sea the red boxes in the hold are packed with fish and ice. Biggi does not sell his catch in Iceland. It will be packed straight into a container bound for

Grimsby, a maritime market town on the north-east coast of England.

As far as Icelanders are concerned, Grimsby and neighbouring Hull are the most important English towns. London is a distant third.

Like Costa Rican coffee, Argentine beef and Canadian maple syrup, the origin of Icelandic fish is a stamp of quality. It travels all over the world, well integrated in a global trade network. Since 1990 Iceland has joined another network, in which footballers are the commodity and those from Iceland are the catch of the day.

## Chapter Six
# Joining the network

HALLDÓR HALLDÓRSSON was 18 years old when he delivered a perceptive judgement of London: 'There are far too many people here.'

It was January 1950 and the young inside-right was on his way to Lincoln City for a two-month trial. Lincoln had played Valur six months earlier on a pre-season tour to Reykjavík and young Halldór made a good enough impression to seal an invitation to England. He enjoyed the journey from London to Lincoln. He had never travelled by train before. Nor had he ever seen so many trees.

But his stay was brief. Halldór did not make an appearance for Lincoln, then of the Third Division North, and presumably returned to Iceland when the two months were up. He wanted to get Stanley Matthews's autograph before he left. It is unknown if he succeeded.

Halldór embarked on his adventure when Iceland was on the periphery, not just geographically, but also as a footballing nation.

Apart from that brief spell during the Second World War, when a fantasy football collection of professional footballers served in the British forces that occupied Iceland, the nation was isolated from the game. English football was rationed on television. From the 1960s onwards, grainy footage of short shorts and sideburns appeared on Icelandic screens every week, but matches were only broadcasted the weekend after they were played. The commentators, having seen the action before the public, flaunted their suspicious ability to predict goals, fouls and free kicks before they happened.

For the first nine decades of the 20th century, Iceland was on the outside of European football, peering in. Few Icelandic players forged careers abroad. The national team was made up of amateur players from the domestic league.

In contrast to British football, however, Iceland was not wilfully insular. It has always been an outward-looking country. The original settlers voyaged to Iceland because of a sense of adventure and curiosity. Viking Europe was well connected to the global trade network, and Iceland – although geographically marginal – was part of this. It is telling that Tara Carter, an American archaeologist, has even written a book on this period titled *Iceland's Networked Society*.

Icelanders emigrated to North America – and as far south as Brazil in the case of Kristján Guðmundsson and his four companions – from the 1860s onwards. Yet even those who stayed in rural Iceland were not as isolated from global affairs as one might imagine. The social historian Sigurður Gylfi Magnússon found the diary of a farmhand from the remote north-west of the country that described the 1904 Russo–Japanese War in remarkable detail. The flow of students around Europe was a chief reason for Iceland remaining in the loop. Inquisitive Icelanders travelled all over the continent and wrote home with news of foreign affairs.

But footballers did not traditionally form part of this stream of emigrants. As a consequence, Iceland was ideologically detached from continental Europe, the hub of global football.

Simon Kuper and Stefan Szymanski – a journalist and economist respectively – would argue that the end of this detachment from Europe helps explain the sharp ascent of Icelandic football. Shortly before the 2010 World Cup, Kuper and Szymanski released a book called *Why England Lose*. A central focus is the perceived underachievement of the England football team. The co-authors present three main explanations. First, England internationals play lots of demanding matches in the Premier League, which saps their energy for international football. Second, an anti-intellectual streak excludes the middle class. Third, England isolated itself from the European knowledge network.

The final point about knowledge networks is relevant to Iceland. For Kuper and Szymanski, networks help explain why some countries perform better at football than others. 'England's problem until recently,' they wrote, 'was probably geography. The country was too far from the networks of continental Europe, where the best football was played.' If England was too far from the networks, then Iceland was off the map.

Knowledge spreads quickly through European football because it is highly integrated. The best players in the world congregate in Spain, England, Italy, Germany and France. Elite clubs from these countries play each other in the Champions League. New ideas about how the game should be played emerge and evolve and spread.

Countries on the periphery miss out on that and, as a result, often develop idiosyncratic and dysfunctional styles of play. English football, for example, was wedded to a 4-4-2 formation and a fondness for putting the ball 'in the mixer' – an infatuation that endured until the rejuvenating influx of foreign coaches, players and expertise in the 1990s. Peripheral countries become attached to bad habits and resist new ideas. Kuper and Szymanski claim this is why those countries tend to underperform.

Kuper and Szymanski use the example of Spain to elaborate. Spain used to be isolated – not geographically, but politically. General Francisco Franco ruled a fascist dictatorship from 1936 until his death in 1975. Spain had a good football team before Franco rose to power. In the four decades that followed, however, Franco reduced Spain's connections to the rest of western Europe. The flow of footballing knowledge stagnated. Fresh ideas turned back at the foothills of the Pyrenees. Spain won the nascent European Nations' Cup – a precursor to the European Championship – on home soil in 1964 but this was an anomaly in a period of mediocrity.

Things changed after the death of Franco. Madrid pulsed to the bacchanalian beat of *La Movida*. Spain opened up again and the flow of footballing nous resumed. In Barcelona the impact was particularly seismic. Johan Cruyff, a Dutchman, crafted a style of play at Barça based on the primacy of the pass and the interpretation of space on the pitch. Spain joined the European Union in 1986, and 20 years later the national team began a cycle of success that yielded the European Championships in 2008 and 2012 and the World Cup in 2010. Spain achieved this using the tiki-taka brand of possession football that had a clear genealogical line back to Cruyff.

Kuper and Szymanski put it pithily: 'Spain became a great football nation because it joined the European knowledge network.'

Iceland joined the European knowledge network in the 1990s. Two events prompted this integration. First, Iceland became a member of the European Economic Area (EEA) in 1994. Second, the Bosman ruling opened the doors of mainland Europe to Icelandic footballers.

The EEA – otherwise known as the single market – is an extension of the European Union. Iceland, Liechtenstein and Norway are members of the EEA but not the EU. These countries, though, are still bound by the 'four freedoms' that underpin the European project: the free movement of goods, services, capital and people. Membership of the EEA was the culmination of a process of Icelandic political integration with Europe that began with the controversial decision to join NATO in 1949, which provoked riots in Reykjavík, and continued with membership of the European Free Trade Association in 1970.

There remains a fundamental tension in Iceland's relationship with Europe. It dates back to the struggle for independence from Denmark in the 19th century. Independence was one strand of the struggle. The other was a desire for economic prosperity. This dichotomy still defines Icelandic politics. Iceland needs access to the European market to deliver the prosperity it craves. But the EU simultaneously threatens that powerful sense of independence.

Eiríkur Bergmann, an expert in European integration and national identity at Bifröst University, believes joining the EEA was a vital step for Iceland.

'Iceland was coming of age at the time,' he says on the phone from a holiday rental in the south of France. 'It paved the way for Icelandic economic integration with European countries. That started immediately and Iceland saw a massive spike in internal growth and there was a prolonged boom in trade.

'Iceland would have been much more economically backwards today if it had not joined the EEA. It was absolutely vital because of the access to the market we desperately needed. Between 70 and 80 per cent of the Icelandic economy is within the European Union.'

Iceland lagged behind much of western Europe and had the foibles to prove it. Television screens went blank every Thursday and throughout the month of July so broadcasters could have some time off. This lasted until 1986. Remarkably, beer was illegal until 1989. Iceland modernised rapidly within the EEA as economic growth combined with the need to comply with European standards and regulations.

As Iceland became more prosperous, Icelandic football improved. It was a natural consequence. A prosperous country can afford to build the infrastructure and social provisions that make football accessible. Moreover, football fell increasingly within the sphere of European jurisdiction in the 1990s, and so the game was dragged along in the wake of change. Iceland was allowed to know what was happening in football. The KSÍ received correspondence from FIFA and UEFA that only applied to nations bound by EU regulations.

The second transformative event of the 1990s was the Bosman ruling. In 1995 the European Court of Justice ruled, in the name of a modest Belgian footballer called Jean-Marc Bosman, that a club could not retain an out-of-contract player if they offered him a new contract on equal terms because it contravened European laws on restraint of trade. Crucially for Icelandic players, restrictions on the number of EU players at a club were also abandoned. As a freshly anointed member of the EEA, the rules applied to Iceland.

Previously, European clubs were allowed to field three non-national players plus three 'assimilated' players who had resided in the country for five years. This created a funnel that limited the emigration of talented Icelandic footballers. Many sought to move to mainland Europe – and were good enough to do so – but there were few non-national squad places for them to occupy. The Bosman ruling cleared that blockage because players from within the EU and EEA were not considered foreigners in employment law.

More Icelandic players could experience professional football. This was not always in the heart of the European knowledge network – Icelandic players migrate to Sweden more than to any other country – but they moved closer to the action than they had been in Iceland. Every time an Icelandic player returned from their professional club

– either for international duty or to see out their career at home – they bore knowledge that had not previously existed in semi-professional Iceland. Ideas about nutrition, conditioning and rehabilitation arrived. So exposure to professional football benefited not only the players who directly experienced it, but Icelandic football as a whole. The appointment of Lars Lagerbäck fits within this paradigm shift. He brought foreign expertise in a managerial capacity.

The Bosman ruling opened a two-way street. More foreign players have populated the Icelandic leagues over the last two decades. English is the dominant language on pitches as far down the pyramid as the Fourth Division. The accents lilt from eastern European to Spanish to American.

Many of these footballing immigrants are players of pedigree. Take Todor Hristov, a Bulgarian, as an example. Since 2015 he has played for Einherji in the Third Division and supplemented his wages by working in a fish factory. Todor spent the 2011/12 season with Levski Sofia, a club with 26 league titles and the first Bulgarian team to qualify for the Champions League group stage. He brings experience that was scarce at Iceland's biggest clubs in the 1980s but is now common as low as the Third Division.

While this diverse tapestry upsets the self-sufficient instincts of some Icelandic football fans, there is little doubt that the presence of foreign players has enhanced the domestic game.

Icelandic footballers themselves now have greater access to the international labour market, and many leave the country at a very young age. According to the Football

Observatory (CIES), members of the Iceland squad at the 2018 World Cup migrated abroad at an average age of 19.05. Only the Belgians moved abroad earlier. But is this a good thing?

'Iceland's figures were crushing. Nobody else was even close to it.'

Gregg Broughton gesticulates as animatedly as the glass of red wine in his hand allows. He personifies Iceland's connection to the European knowledge network. When Gregg became the head of academy recruitment at Norwich City in 2012, he began to comb Iceland for teenage talent. He recalls the process over dinner at a harbourside restaurant in Bodø, Norway, where he now works at Bodø/Glimt.

Gregg and his colleagues applied statistical methodology to player recruitment. They wanted to know which areas of England produced the most professional footballers. Norwich is a small provincial city that cannot provide enough young players to fill a competitive academy, so they needed to look further afield. South-east and north-east London emerged as the most fertile terrain for footballers within commutable distance of Norwich. Now, several years after the advent of that clinical process, a player making the transition to the Norwich first team is as likely to hail from East Ham as East Anglia.

When Gregg expanded academy recruitment to Europe, Iceland rose to the top of the spreadsheet for producing professional footballers. Another report from the Football Observatory vindicates his methodology. It found in 2018 that the country with the highest rate of expatriate footballers per million of inhabitants was Iceland (180).

Montenegro (134) was the only other country with a figure above 100. The use of 'per capita' has become wincingly clichéd as a framing device for Icelandic sporting achievement. But, in this instance, it is the clearest way to articulate Iceland's flair for football husbandry. This is why scouts flock to Reykjavík.

Gregg added further criteria to the study of Europe: how many players from each country returned home shortly after joining a foreign club? How many signed contract extensions? Again, Iceland performed well. When Icelandic players move abroad they tend to assimilate. Relatively few fail to adapt or suffer from insurmountable homesickness.

'Icelandic players are very adaptable because Icelanders want to move and experience life abroad,' Gregg theorises. 'It doesn't matter if you're a footballer or you work in business.'

A thirst for the horizon forms an important part of the Icelandic identity. *Heimskur* is the Icelandic word for 'someone who stays at home', but it also means 'stupid'. Travel is a pre-condition of intelligence in Iceland. Traditionally, it was also a reality of the labour market. Farmers flocked to the coast for the fishing season, leaving the farm in the hands of their wife and children. Urban dwellers travelled to the countryside each summer to bolster the farmhand workforce during the busiest months of the year. Moving from place to place is part of Icelandic culture.

In addition to the attractive character traits of Icelandic footballers, the market appealed to Gregg because of its modest size.

'That was important for Norwich,' he says between forkfuls of breaded cod. 'Our scouting network and budget were small compared to other clubs. If we wanted to find the best player in France it would have been like looking for a needle in a haystack. And if we did find him, we would be fighting with PSG, Real Madrid and Bayern Munich. In Iceland we didn't feel we would face the same competition.'

Gregg began to establish relationships with the right people in Iceland. He delivered seminars to Icelandic coaches through the KSÍ, and Norwich agreed to send teams to the Rey Cup, an annual tournament held in Reykjavík for under-14 and under-16 teams. From January 2013 Norwich scouts were a permanent presence at training camps held to exhibit the best teenagers in the country. Norwich did not just make an impact in Iceland; Iceland had a profound impact on Gregg. Months spent scouring for rough diamonds exposed him to the menacing beauty of the island. He chose the Snæfellsnes peninsula, where volcanoes and glacier meet the sea, as the setting to propose to his fiancée.

Norwich were in the market for 14- and 15-year-old players who could sign after their 16th birthday. The going rate was between £20,000 and £50,000. Gregg had to persevere. Norwich missed out on his targets from the 1998 and 1999 groups – in reference to their year of birth – to Reading and FC Twente, clubs with deep roots in Iceland. Ágúst Hlynsson, a playmaker from Breiðablik, was the breakthrough. Ajax, Stuttgart and Cologne had identified him. Ágúst's father had concerns about his son's suitability to the hard running and hard tackles of the English game.

'We felt our major selling point was Norwich's geographical isolation,' Gregg says. 'The training ground is very rural. Going from Reykjavík to London, or even Birmingham, can be a huge culture change.' Norwich was a bigger pond than Iceland. But not too big, not overwhelmingly big.

Two more midfielders – Ísak Þorvaldsson and Atli Barkarson – arrived in Norwich the following year. 'All of a sudden,' Gregg says, 'we felt we were ahead of all other English clubs in the Icelandic market. Norwich had a really big name in the area.'

The signing of Atli Barkarson reveals much about the astonishing range of the European network. He is from Húsavík, a town of 2,000 souls on the northern shores of Iceland with a far stronger reputation for whale watching than football. Atli played in the Third Division for his local side, IF Völsungur, before he joined Norwich. A club from the extreme east of England was able to identify and sign a teenager from the extreme north of Iceland.

Ágúst left Norwich without making a first-team appearance and is now back in Iceland after a spell in Denmark. Gregg acknowledges that the club did not create a clear pathway for him to progress, as fellow youngsters James Maddison and Todd Cantwell occupied his favoured position behind the striker. Atli left for Fredrikstad in Norway, while Ísak joined Fleetwood Town in January 2020 after consistent performances for Norwich under-23s. The mixed fortunes of the trio show that a move abroad is not a guarantee of a professional career. Young footballers must negotiate a talent funnel as they pass from their teens to their twenties, when the budding players far outnumber the contracts on the table. It is inevitable that some Icelanders will get stuck. Unlike most players, however, the Icelanders have already made the sacrifice of leaving their country.

A talented and adaptable pool of players was not enough on its own to make Iceland a viable market for Norwich or other clubs from major European leagues. Two other conditions had to be ripe. First, Icelandic clubs had to be willing to negotiate. Second, and above all, the agents needed to be tame.

Brian Clough was never short of a zinging remark, and agents did not escape his acerbic tongue. In his superb biography of Clough, *Provided You Don't Kiss Me*, Duncan Hamilton recalls a nostalgic conversation held towards the end of Clough's tenure at Nottingham Forest. They reminisced about the 1970s, simpler times.

'The only agent back then was 007,' Clough quipped. 'And he just shagged women, not entire football clubs.'

Agents are cast as a scar on the face of football. Their influence has ballooned in tandem with their clients' wages. Clough captured the essence of their presentation in popular discourse: they are leeches, duplicitous and sly. The reality is rather more mundane in Iceland, where a handful of dependable agents are operational.

Ólafur Garðarsson and Bjarki Gunnlaugsson are two of the agents who pave the route for Icelandic players to test themselves in bigger European leagues, often before they have experienced first-team football in Iceland.

With a well-cut suit and a side-parting, Ólafur has the sartorial air of a Wall Street wolf. He is a lawyer by trade. These days he only does legal work for a small selection of long-term clients. Football demands most of his time and covers the walls in his clean-cut office, where photos of his clients peer down. He became a football agent in the days when the deposit of a princely sum in a Swiss bank account was sufficient to secure a licence. Jóhann Birnir Guðmundsson was the first player Ólafur moved out of Iceland. He joined Watford in 1998. Graham Taylor, the Watford manager at the time, stuck pins in a map of Iceland to mark the locations of players that might be of interest.

A framed letter on the wall stands out from the photographs. The green letterhead and embossed '96' betray its origin as the Bundesliga club Hannover 96. It is from the managing director. 'I have been in this business for several years now and known many agents,' the letter reads. 'That one of them has been so engaged for one of his players and therefore a transfer, as well as spending so much time and energy on it, I have rarely seen.'

Ólafur proudly curates his reputation for scrupulousness. So it comes as a surprise that he advocates slacker regulations concerning the transfer of under-16 players.

'A 15-year-old boy is not allowed to go abroad to play football,' he says with a wry smile and his palms open. 'Let's say I have a 15-year-old boy and Brøndby want him. The father and mother want him to go. His Icelandic club want to let him go. Brøndby want to buy him. He even has a sister in Denmark and he will live with her. Where is the crime?'

Ólafur understands the intention of FIFA's regulations is to prevent the exploitation of children from third-world countries, who are lured to Europe with false promises of a contract and are promptly abandoned. Yet he calls for nuance, for different rules for transfers between, for example, two Nordic nations, where the likelihood of manipulation is slim. Ólafur's fundamental belief is that players should leave Iceland in their teenage years, not just to further their football education, but to expand their boundaries through life abroad.

Bjarki Gunnlaugsson agrees. A former midfielder for Feyenoord, Preston North End and, on five separate occasions, hometown club ÍA Akranes, he is a co-founder of Total Football, an agency representing around 40 Icelandic players. A canvas of Eiður Guðjohnsen in a Barcelona shirt, the Champions League trophy cradled in his arms, dominates one wall of Total Football's office, a floor-to-ceiling-window affair above a seafood restaurant in the quaint part of Reykjavík.

'The more players that go abroad, the better it will be for the national team,' Bjarki reasons. He embraces amicable coexistence with Ólafur on the altruistic basis that the Icelandic game benefits from more contacts and wider networks.

In September 2019, Total Football became part of Stellar Group – the sports management company founded by Gareth Bale's agent, Jonathan Barnett – and rebranded as Stellar Nordic. It was a natural progression for an agency that sought to give its clients opportunities across Europe. And, in joining the Stellar behemoth, Bjarki and his colleagues showed that all components of Icelandic football, right up to the agents that move the players, are constantly moving closer to European networks.

A whiteboard covers the wall behind Bjarki's desk. Players who are already abroad occupy one half. Players still in Iceland are on the other. Some are as young as 14. While Bjarki does not have a contractual relationship with players of that age, he tracks their progress through teenage tumult. Burly senior players often stand in their way. For Bjarki, this is both a frustration and a justification for ushering the best young players to mainland Europe.

'I once said in an interview with Icelandic radio that if Lionel Messi had been born in Iceland he would not have played for a first team when he was young, because he was small. Maybe I was exaggerating but that's the way we think: it's a physical game here so you need to have physical players.'

Bjarki is expounding the technical qualities of the cohort born in 2002 and 2003 when the door opens and a gangly teenager enters. Skinny jeans accentuate wiry legs. They talk in Icelandic for five minutes.

'This guy is a little caught in between at Fulham,' Bjarki explains after he has left. 'He won't ever play for the first team there. He's only 19. It's no age. But he has to be ready to take a step back in order to take two steps forwards.' In practical terms that means a move to Scandinavia and a platform from which to plot a different path to the big leagues. This was the case for the two players who left Norwich, and so it transpired for their compatriot at Fulham. The player joined a Danish side on loan in the summer of 2018 and was in the senior Iceland squad by the autumn.

'My feeling with players is that the glass is always half-empty,' Bjarki continues. He is speaking generally now, not just about the boy at Fulham. 'They tend to think the coach is being mean to them, the grass is too green, the sun is too bright, the sky is too blue, whatever. They never look at themselves and I was probably the same when I was playing. It's just human. But in the end they have to realise there is no conspiracy.'

This frank admission begs the question of whether footballers have the emotional skills to move abroad at the age of 16. It is a quandary that raises issues about a duty of care.

Players can either stay or go. They cannot do both. And there is no right or wrong path. Ólafur, who facilitated Gylfi Sigurðsson's move to Reading, concedes that some players are 'a little bit broken' when a move turns sour.

'But when do you know if they're emotionally ready?' he contends. 'It's every boy's dream to go abroad but it's never just wine and roses. The difficult times come when the coach is being difficult. You're living in digs in England and you have to be careful what you tell the host family because everything you tell them goes back to the club. Sometimes the whole family moves with the boy. If a family can do that for the first year, year and a half, two years, that's very important.

'You're hardly a worse player if you have to come back to Iceland after three years,' he adds. 'You sometimes learn another language, you live away from Iceland and away from home for a couple of years, which is always good. It broadens your horizons.'

Jón Rúnar Halldórsson is not so sure. He made FH the most successful Icelandic club of the 21st century before stepping down as chairman in 2019, and is adamant the agents underestimate the emotional damage that a failed spell abroad can inflict on a teenager.

'Those guys, the agents, they don't know what I'm talking about. They don't understand it. They say they are always thinking about the player but they are not, they are partially thinking of their own salaries.'

Jón Rúnar is thickset with salt-and-pepper cropped hair. In a deep voice that is at once emollient and ominous, he tells me that his association with FH goes back 60 years. His wife refers to the club as the mistress in their marriage.

When a foreign club tables an offer for one of his teenage players, Jón Rúnar proposes an initial loan move that all parties can choose to make permanent after six months or a year. 'If things go wrong, he can come back home from a loan, which is totally different to a broken contract. He can come home like this' – he puffs out his chest – 'rather than like this' – he hunches his shoulders.

Jón Rúnar speaks in measured sentences, straight and pointed like arrows. 'We are very good at exporting fish. But what were we always doing? We were exporting raw materials. We have now discovered that people in Europe are frying herring. We never knew because we were just exporting it. Come on!

'We need to do it differently. I believe that. Sport is all about getting better, new victories, higher mountains to climb. If we don't take care of our best and try to improve the club level here to compete with the Danish, you can close the shop and say goodbye.'

Jón Rúnar is a provocateur. 'We don't like the FA,' he says with a smile that indicates he is playing up to a reputation for contrarianism. He believes the KSÍ is too controlling and that it should devolve more power to the clubs. He also detects a self-congratulatory tone at the KSÍ on account of the success of the national team. This chafes with his conviction that the health of the clubs – and their progress in UEFA competitions – is a more reliable barometer of the national game than the national team. 'We are rebels,' he smiles. 'We are very often against the establishment.'

Yet Jón Rúnar is a draconian figure in the eyes of some of the more modest clubs. His vision to keep the best Icelandic players in Iceland for longer relies on smaller clubs' acquiescence to more powerful institutions. He advocates a joint academy to allow the best players to train together throughout the winter. This would inevitably lead to the stockpiling of talent at five or six gatekeeper clubs.

'We need to focus on doing better,' he insists, 'so a 17-year-old doesn't need to go because he thinks he will be better trained elsewhere. Make that happen here. We need to work together. It's better to have our players training in an academy, trying to prolong their stay here so they don't go to academies in Holland or wherever when they are 16 or 17.'

But for whom is it better? The players? Or patricians like Jón Rúnar, who has a duty to protect the interests of his club?

Integration with the European knowledge network has come at the price of conflict at club level. The top Icelandic clubs strive to reach the group stage of the Europa League, or even the Champions League. This gold-rush mentality encourages short-termism, which is not easily compatible with an emphasis on developing local talent. Icelandic clubs may be semi-professional but the coaches are still judged on results. Most will favour a wily professional from Denmark over a raw talent from Reykjavík. Young players know this, and it makes the path to the mainland more enticing. Footballers are no different from the generations of Icelanders who, frustrated by a lack of opportunities at home, crossed the waves of the Atlantic in search of education and adventure.

## Chapter Seven
# Size matters

SIGGI BALDURSSON looks every bit the veteran percussionist. He leans back on a creaking office chair. A pair of bongo drums straddles his thighs. He pats the skin with thumb, little finger, thumb, little finger until he sees me. He rests his palm on the drum. 'Tea?' he offers.

Blown-up images from the Iceland Airwaves festival decorate this open-plan office on the corner of Hlemmur Square. The bus station at the centre of the square has been converted into a trendy food hall but the yellow single-deckers still heave past the door.

Siggi flicks on the kettle and suggests a game of ping-pong on the orange table that acts as the focal point of the room. I explain the concept of my book while wondering how he manages to generate such devilish topspin.

Siggi is a well-known figure in the Icelandic music scene, although the tight-knit nature of the scene means everyone is relatively well known. Siggi was part of the punk scene that blossomed in the early 1980s. His face is round and ruddy, nothing like the punk pastiness associated with safety-pin-through-the-ear anaemia. His eyes twinkle behind thin-rimmed glasses as he reminisces. 'Back in those days we were underground kids from Reykjavík. We were not in popular pop bands; we didn't play the school parties and country dances and stuff like that. We were into *art*, quote unquote.'

Siggi emerged from the underground as the drummer in The Sugarcubes, the alternative rock band that thrust Björk into the limelight. They were the darlings of the *NME* in an era when the English musical press could act as a trampoline for obscure artists. Siggi now runs Iceland Music – a promotional agency for Icelandic musicians – from this bohemian office.

On the side he is still involved with Bad Taste (*Smekkleysa* in Icelandic), a non-profit record label established in 1986 to incubate sounds that were viable artistically if not commercially.

The American military base at Keflavík inspired Icelandic rock music. 'The American forces radio was the most defining element,' Siggi explains. 'We were all listening to American forces radio. Keflavík became known as "Rock City". That was where the first "popular" pop bands came from. It was rock 'n' roll, basically.'

The kettle boils. Siggi brews green tea in a china pot and we settle on a table that wobbles enough to distract but not enough for either of us to do anything about it.

Siggi remembers a name and chuckles to himself. Rúnar Júlíusson, a rock star. Keflavík was his stage in the early 1970s. He also played football for Iceland and married the Icelandic beauty queen. 'All at the same time,' Siggi marvels. 'He was a gentleman's gentleman.'

The echoes of that era still reverberate through the PA system on matchdays in Keflavík. That is where the best half-time playlist in Iceland blasts out, curated by indie kid Björn from his cosy booth on the halfway line.

It might seem strange to talk about music in a book about football, but there are surprising similarities: the conditions that allow Iceland to punch above its weight in music are also the source of much of Iceland's footballing success.

The Sugarcubes and Björk emerged from Reykjavík to achieve global acclaim in the 1980s and 1990s. Sigur Rós, Múm, Of Monsters and Men and Kaleo followed. Icelandic musical émigrés have also flourished beyond the basecamp genres of rock and alternative. The composer Jóhann Jóhannsson, who died tragically in 2018, received an Oscar nomination in 2015 for his work on the soundtrack for the Stephen Hawking biopic, *The Theory of Everything*. Hildur Guðnadóttir, who used to share a studio with Jóhannsson, won an Oscar for her composition of the score for *Joker*, released in 2019.

There are items that sit firmly in the centre of the Venn diagram of music and football. For instance, local authorities subsidise young people to pursue music and sport. Every municipality in Iceland is obliged to fund a music school. As a result, there are 87 such schools across the country, with an estimated 12,000 students enrolled at any one time. Lilja Alfreðsdóttir – the Icelandic Minister of Education, Science, and Culture – explains the rationale: 'If you look at philosophers like Socrates, he put emphasis on music and sports. You need exercise in order to feel good and have certain self-esteem, and it's the same with music. It helps you harmonise and value information. His writings are applicable today and it's for these exact reasons that we subsidise sports and music.'

Music and football in Iceland share another commonality: they both benefit from Iceland being a small nation. First, because smallness is conducive to the swift exchange of knowledge. Second, because the impact of positive role models is amplified in a small country.

Siggi pours a pale stream of tea from a height. 'In smaller societies you have a psychological meandering that goes on. People constantly believe they can do things and there's more of a team effort. "What do we need to do this? OK, let's get our shit together. I'll do this, you do that, let's organise." That's an interesting element if you look at it from a sociological point of view. We always talk about "per capita" because we get away with all sorts of shit here if you look at it per capita.'

The relationship between population and achievement is misunderstood, he opines: 'We're always led to believe that success in arts and sports is a selective process. That's why the Russians are so good at skiing, or whatever. If you filter down you'll find three super skiers because there are so many of them. But you can create some serious competition in a small place if you just focus on it.

'There is something about the focus and single-mindedness of how people do things here that creates good musicians and good sportsmen. I also think it's an element of idiot savant.'

He takes my pen and scribbles a phrase in Icelandic. *Huginn ber mig hálfa leið.*

'It's an Icelandic saying from the old days. It means "The mind will carry you halfway there." If you believe you can actually do something, you've got a good head start. You need to have that belief that you are actually going to succeed. That's what I call idiot savant. It makes sense. "I don't know any better, so why shouldn't I succeed at this? Why not?"'

This is what Viðar Halldórsson, a sociologist at the University of Iceland, calls the 'Icelandic Madness'. He defines it as a collective identity, shared by Icelandic sports teams, shaped by the belief that an Icelander can do anything if they see an end goal and play with their hearts as well as their heads. The infectious confidence that the Icelandic football team secrete is symptomatic of the 'madness'.

'That plays very strongly in the Icelandic character, how I understand it having lived abroad for long periods of time,' Siggi continues. 'If we allow ourselves the luxury of generalising, there is definitely a funny aspect to this Icelandic character. There's a lot of ambition and a lot of belief that we can actually get away with all sorts of shit.

'I think that's why they call us the Italians of the North. We seem to have this need to bend the rules. I think that's historical. This nation grows out of a farming and fishing culture, which demands that you go out and do shit when it's possible to do so. When the fish are swimming you have to go out and get them. When the sun is up you have to cut the grass and dry it. That carves into people's mentalities over a period of time. You feel you can bend the rules. That mentality can be very good if you're in the creative industries. But it's probably very bad if you're a banker.'

He pauses while the wires in his brain make connections and spark. 'There is a very creative element in football as well, which is partially what makes it interesting.'

Örvar Smárason – a founding member of Múm, an experimental group formed in Reykjavík in 1997 – believes that creative element is what binds football and music above all else. 'Football is all about creating something,' he says. 'It's about moments of chaos within a structure. That's something both footballers and musicians need to have, and they need to have it constantly, not just once.'

Retirement beckons for those who can no longer summon that spontaneity. 'This is why you see footballers hit a wall. They seem tired but I don't think it's just their legs that go after another long season. It's also a burnout of the creative spark. It's unquantifiable. It's hard to put your finger on that spark, therefore it's hard to get it back.'

While Icelandic football and music both rely on resourcefulness to overachieve, there is a difference in the aesthetic of the outcome. The musicians pride themselves on being innovative, or even unique, in their pursuit of a beautiful sound. Few people would argue, on the other hand, that Iceland play football that is innovative or conventionally attractive. It is based on structure and discipline rather than flair. But even if the style of play does not facilitate individual creativity, Iceland has to be creative to get 11 good players on the pitch in the first place. Music and football rely on similar creative processes that lead to very different outcomes.

Örvar is a football obsessive with a tattoo to prove it. The Valur crest is inked on the inside of his right bicep. He has recently returned from a trip to Istanbul to watch Beşiktaş when we meet in a Reykjavík coffee house. A structured interview quickly disintegrates into a conversation between two anoraks. Yet talking about music does not come naturally to Örvar.

'It kind of bores me,' he sighs. 'It's often about a side of music that seems natural to journalists but makes less and less sense to me. They're thinking about it from the outside. When you're actually doing the work and seeing it from the inside, it sometimes feels fake to talk about it like that. But if I was a professional footballer I would probably think everyone was talking shit and creating a narrative around me.'

Sunday League football was Örvar's level, until his knee went. And while he may not talk freely about music in itself, the parallels with football interest him.

'You need to lay the foundations for everything. You need to put yourself in a situation where creativity takes over. In football the physical work, tactical work, technical work is all to put yourself in that situation where the little spark can take over. It's similar to music in so many ways, but people only see the top layer of things. Things like hope and passion often fit better into the narrative, so creativity is overlooked.'

For many Icelandic musicians, the foundations of creativity that Örvar refers to take the form of a tight community underpinned by collaboration and support. Nick Prior – a sociologist from the University of Edinburgh – argues that tight-knit networks are the best way to explain the number of successful Icelandic musicians. In a 2015 study titled 'It's a Social Thing, Not a Nature Thing', Prior lamented the misconception that all Icelandic musicians draw inspiration from the natural environment. 'It is rare to find a review of the Icelandic post-rock band Sigur Rós that does not describe their music as "glacial",' he rued.

Björk is a high-profile example of an artist who does draw inspiration from the trees and tundra, as shown by her *Biophilia* project that started life in 2010 as a concept album made up of ten tracks with links to the natural world. Most musicians, however, mention the Reykjavík 'scene' when asked about their inspiration. Prior sees an intimacy in the scene that he refers to as 'Village-like'. Everyone knows everyone. Genres merge as artists share instruments, equipment and the limited rehearsal spaces.

Siggi has seen Prior's 'Village-like properties' in action across several decades. 'There is a lot of bleed between genres. I think they call it "cross-pollination" between sectors and style types. It makes for a very creative community. You have people from the contemporary music scene collaborating with the metal scene, who also collaborate with people from the electronic scene, the indie-rock scene or the jazz scene. I'm not saying it's all a big mix; there are very distinct scenes here. But there is movement between them that we don't normally see in bigger communities.'

Siggi is unequivocal about the root of such healthy musical collaboration. 'It's because of the smallness of the community. The music community is exceptionally creative and active – they're spewing out more creative, interesting music per capita than anywhere else in the world – but it's also quite small and tight.'

Jón Jónsson is not like Siggi or Örvar. He is a pop star without pretensions. He did not spend his youth getting lost in Led Zeppelin through a haze of sweet smoke. 'Give me a Coldplay CD and I'm happy,' he quips. Jón is a familiar face in Iceland, and not just for his easy-listening music. He presents the Icelandic coverage of the Eurovision Song Contest and, until he retired in January 2018, played football at the highest level in Iceland. He spent most of his career at FH and won the Icelandic title in 2012 and 2015. Incidentally, his father is Jón Rúnar Halldórsson.

Although Jón is not, to use his own words, 'artsy', he appreciates the inclusivity of the music scene. 'What is beautiful about the scene is how small it is. And even though it's competitive, people are still willing to help each other. There are lots of people playing in different bands. The same guys are recording and producing all the stuff.

'That really helps when it comes to the exchange of knowledge. Sometimes it's just in the subconscious. Let's say that one time you play with a new drummer and he does something cool. You'd be like, "Hey, this is nice." The drummer isn't saying, "We should do this." But you pick it up.'

Most people view smallness as detrimental to producing talent. Admittedly, if we were to create a country ideally suited for success in international football, we would fill it with more inhabitants than are scattered across Iceland. The discourse around Icelandic football, as with music, marvels that a small nation can flourish but overlooks the ways in which smallness contributes to that success.

While Icelandic football benefited from moving closer to the European knowledge network in the 1990s, it also benefits from the tight networks that can only exist in a small community. Take Icelandic youth coaching as an example. Heads of youth from every Icelandic club convene at monthly meetings organised by the KSÍ. They have a platform to exchange ideas and discuss the common problems they face. Their coaching philosophies blend like jazz and rap in the dingy rehearsal rooms of Reykjavík.

These meetings would not be possible in a bigger country, where logistics and bureaucracy restrict collaboration. Indeed, the KSÍ's entire approach to coach education is bathed in the principles of inclusivity and outreach to isolated parts of the country. If a budding coach cannot travel to Reykjavík for a course, the course travels to the coach. This only works because the community of coaches is small enough to manage centrally.

Former technical director of the KSÍ, Siggi Eyjólfsson, sculpted a holistic approach to coach education in Iceland. He has since worked in China, most recently as the head coach of the women's national team. There are innumerable differences between Iceland and China, but Eyjólfsson homes in on two. First, the demographics could scarcely be more different: according to the 2010 Chinese census, there are 201 cities in China with a population greater than that of Iceland. Second, football infrastructure in China lags behind Iceland, where the game is stitched into the fabric of society.

If he were in charge of plotting the course of Chinese football, Eyjólfsson's solution would be to reduce China to a constellation of smaller networks. If the Chinese government and football authorities were to designate one 'football city' with a population of, say, four million, it would be easier to create infrastructure and establish a culture there than across a sprawling nation of 1.4 billion.

The premise at the heart of Eyjólfsson's theory is that tightening the network can increase cohesion, collaboration and, by extension, performance. Iceland's demography is conducive to a tight internal network, particularly as two-thirds of the meagre population are clustered around the Reykjavík urban area.

It is possible, however, for a country to be too tightly tied. Networks are not inherently beneficial. Grétar Steinsson, chief European scout at Everton, warns that familiarity can stifle frank discussion, as appeasement becomes more important than free speech: 'It's very dangerous to have an opinion in a small nation because you get ridiculed on social media or forums for pointing out what nobody wants to hear.'

A forthright comment can be misconstrued as a personal dig. 'Let's say you offend someone,' Grétar theorises, 'a relative of theirs or someone they went to school with who works in the media. Straight away you need to be treading on eggshells. Sometimes it's best to say, "Nah, I'll leave it" because if I say something my family is going to be brought into it. You need to be very, very careful.

'It's very difficult to have a high-performance culture because everyone is so connected,' he continues. 'Conflict is part of high performance. But if you say something here everyone takes it personally. That's why you don't surround yourself with friends. There needs to be someone in the corner who says, "What about someone else?"'

In Iceland knowledge not only flows within football; the boundaries between different sports are porous. This is a product of the European multi-sport club model that prevails in Iceland. Manchester United is purely a football club, whereas Real Madrid has a successful basketball division and Barcelona's handball team is among the best in Europe.

Freyr Alexandersson – assistant coach of the men's national team and former head coach of the women's – cites a colleague at Valur, where he first coached, as a formative influence. The colleague in question was a handball coach. Opposition analysis in handball is more meticulous than in football. Freyr extracted analysis techniques from his colleague at Valur and applied them to his own sport.

Heimir Hallgrímsson also eschews the benefits of collaboration between coaches of different sports: 'There's such easy access to other sports here. The coaches of other sports are your friends. You meet them and watch handball or basketball. In the end we all get what we want. We all get the best information.'

Iceland will always be collaborative. Given the meagre size of its population it cannot work any other way, and as Heimir and Freyr attest, that is clearly healthy when it comes to drawing inspiration from other sports. But it must collaborate without becoming cliquey. That said, despite Grétar's legitimate concerns, Icelandic football appears to be collaborative in a way that is not restrictive to innovation. The KSÍ has taken bold decisions that may not have been unanimously welcome, such as employing Lars Lagerbäck on a contract that, by Icelandic standards, was extremely generous.

Although Grétar is talking about football, his words also apply to the incestuous corruption and shutting down of legitimate discussion that contributed to the financial crisis in 2008. Football must heed that warning and keep channels of communication open, regardless of whether the opinions that travel through them are hard to accept.

Outside the financial markets, 2008 was a watershed in other, positive, ways. The Icelandic handball team won the silver medal at the Beijing Olympics. Their place on the podium was unprecedented: Iceland had excelled at individual sports – particularly those that involve picking up, throwing or pushing heavy objects – but never at team sports.

Ólafur Stefánsson is the most successful Icelandic handball player in history. A gentle giant at 6ft 5in, he played 318 times for his country across 21 years and won the Icelandic Sports Personality of the Year award four times. His career has taken him to Germany, Spain, Denmark and Qatar. But above all else, he takes pride in that silver medal. Ólafur was the captain of that team.

The Olympians returned to Iceland as national heroes. They cruised through Reykjavík on the back of a flatbed lorry, soaking up applause from crowds who had never had such cause for sporting celebration. In grainy footage of the parade, Ólafur wears a dazed smile above the medal round his neck. He had been imagining the moment for a long time.

When I meet him, his thoughts are overflowing like pennies dropping from the shelf in an arcade. 'I need to start drawing or something,' he says, taking my notepad and pen. 'I usually have my iPad with me. I'm a very visual guy.'

He begins to doodle. His energy flows through the pen and on to the page. His body language relaxes, as if a tap has opened to release the pressure. 'You have mushrooms or plants that are single organisms,' he says frantically, his narration dragged by the pen in his hand. 'You have a whole network for one mushroom that stretches over a larger area. They're all connected. They're all one. But the mushrooms think they are separate because they don't see underneath.'

He looks up as if the point is obvious. I frown. The result of his scribbling is four mushrooms protruding from the earth. They are connected by a network of squiggled roots.

It comes as little surprise that Ólafur dabbles in the esoteric. He applied for a medical degree as a young man. He now self-diagnoses this decision as Freudian – an attempt to follow the path of his absent father, who went to Sweden to pursue a career in medicine. Ólafur spent much of his childhood with his grandfather, a theologian and philosopher. He absorbed anecdotes about values and learned to question everything, to look beyond the apparent.

That denialist streak formed the contours of Ólafur's character as a sportsman. He did not have a reference point for success when he was growing up. Icelandic teams achieved little and, therefore, there was an absence of role models. Instead, Ólafur created them on paper. He repeated the same drawing for years: a cluster of stick figures represented the Iceland national team. They stood on a platform: the Olympic podium. It had one level rather than three because Ólafur did not mind if the medal was gold, silver or bronze.

'If you want a gold medal, it's not just about writing down: "I want this." You have to be a good enough "imaginer" – that's what I call it – to actually be there. You have to know how that state of being would be. That's why it's so easy to bail out or get distracted; you don't feel like you've lost anything because you haven't felt what you were losing.'

He uses the example of the four-minute mile. The target eluded middle-distance runners until 1954, when Roger Bannister – a 25-year-old medical student from England – crossed the line with a time of 3:59.4. Six weeks later an Australian runner called John Landy ran a sub-four-minute mile. Over 1,400 athletes have achieved the feat since. 'When one guy did it everybody came after,' Ólafur says.

Three lines of text accompany his mushroom diagram. The first says 'pure imagination'. The second says 'see = belief'. The third says 'belief = see'.

We often believe things to be impossible because we have never seen them done. Why persevere if there is no evidence that it is possible to succeed? By achieving the sub-four-minute mile, Bannister presented his fellow athletes with evidence that it was attainable.

Ólafur emphasises the importance of role models. He summons another example: in 1997 three Harvard psychologists instructed a group of Asian-American women to complete a mathematics test. The women performed better when the psychologists emphasised their ethnicity and the associated stereotype that Asian people are good with numbers, compared to when the psychologists emphasised their gender and the stereotype that men are better with numbers than women. The experiment showed that social identity can improve – or impede – performance in a mathematics test.

Ólafur argues that cultural capital can have a similar effect in sport. 'If you come from a club or country that has no story of success, you identify yourself with that. Where nothing has ever happened, nothing will happen. But if, as an Icelander, you can relate to someone who has achieved something, something more will happen.'

The silver medal in 2008 carved a path through the mediocrity that the stars of the future could tread. It created a stereotype of sporting success that had not previously existed but that current and future athletes could identify with. The effect of this is amplified in Iceland, where most people have a social or familial link to one of the athletes.

'Maybe what happened in 2008 gave Icelanders something to relate to,' he muses. 'Handball isn't that big, but it's the Olympics and it's a medal. They're Icelandic, I'm Icelandic. Maybe that's enough. Maybe that triggered or opened something.'

A year after the Olympics, the Iceland women's football team qualified for the European Championship to become the first senior football team from Iceland to feature in a major tournament. Two years after that, the men's under-21 side also qualified for a continental competition, an event that marked the maturation of the best cohort of players Iceland has produced. Now those players have become influential role models, aided by the perception that they are still part of their communities, playing on behalf of their neighbours.

Senior figures within the KSÍ believe that Olympic medal caused a ripple effect that spread to other sports. It fostered confidence and expectation. Football coaches flocked to the handball players and staff to glean information. The handball players also recorded a motivational video for the women's national team before their tournament debut in 2009.

While the proximity of success is a new thing in Icelandic football, it is well established in music, as Siggi Baldursson explains: 'If you're interested in taking your music abroad and you don't personally know someone who has toured internationally, you can bet your uncle knows someone, or your sister's friend knows someone. People have these role models and it plays into the idea of empowerment. People feel that this is a small community. "If she can do it, then yeah, we can do it."'

After 2008, Icelanders did not need to be 'imaginers' like Ólafur. An Icelandic team was succeeding right before their eyes. The silver medal prompted a subtle change in the collective psyche from 'Why us?' to 'Why not us?'

## Chapter Eight
# The coaches

IN SEPTEMBER 2003, Iceland held Germany to a stodgy 0-0 draw at Laugardalsvöllur. Although the visitors had reached the World Cup Final 14 months earlier, the result prompted sombre self-reflection in Germany.

'Iceland are top of the table,' Rudi Völler said on German television. 'You are saying we have to dominate them away from home? What kind of world are you living in? You have to get off your high horse.'

The printed press bemoaned aimless punts to anonymous forwards and Michael Ballack's impotence in midfield. Yet, as Raphael Honigstein explains in *Das Reboot*, sweeping changes were afoot in German football. A painful quarter-final defeat to Croatia in the 1998 World Cup catalysed systematic investment in youth development. Humiliation bred progress. Regional training centres opened from the Black Forest to Berlin. The generation of players who won the World Cup in 2014 were the children of that reform. They benefited from better training, and more of it, than those who came before. As Germany floundered in Reykjavík, the first fruits of the grassroots overhaul – players like Philipp Lahm and Bastian Schweinsteiger – were poised to make an impact.

And in Iceland, as in Germany, radical change simmered just beneath the surface.

'My vision was to improve the level of coaching and expose Icelandic coaches to foreign experts and coaching at a higher level.'

Siggi Eyjólfsson, the former technical director of the KSÍ, leans back against a dune of pillows in his hotel room in Jordan, where the women's Asian Cup is being held. He became the head coach of the China team in 2017 and his words echo through a WeChat connection – Skype is illegal in China.

Eyjólfsson was 29 years old and winding down a nomadic career that took him to the USA, England and Belgium, when the KSÍ appointed him as their first technical director in 2002.

'The KSÍ was very small back then,' he recalls. 'There were maybe ten or 11 people. My office was the meeting room, so I always had to clear my desk when there was going to be a meeting.'

Eyjólfsson's remit was to improve the quality and quantity of Icelandic coaches. He inherited very little. The man previously in charge of coach education juggled the role with a full-time teaching job and leadership of the under-21 national team. There was no structure or syllabus. The budget was meagre. And Iceland, as one of few European nations outside UEFA's coaching convention, remained on the northern periphery of the continent when it came to coach education. Eyjólfsson's first task was to move Iceland closer to its neighbours by adopting the UEFA licensing system, which incorporates, in ascending order of complexity, the B Licence, A Licence and Pro Licence. National associations have certain flexibility to shape each licence to fit their specific needs.

Eyjólfsson had a blank slate to work with. 'We had to design the courses from scratch and decide what we were going to teach at each level. I asked myself: "What is important for the coaches of Iceland to know in order to improve the level of play?"'

He did not rush. He studied a Masters in Sport and Exercise Psychology while playing college soccer in the United States. That instilled an academic respect for the power of patient consideration. He worked as if he would be the technical director for life.

'I'm the type of guy who likes to research things,' he says. 'I like to think about things. To have a really good system you have to put thought into it. If you're always changing and making new policy, you don't follow through with your plan and you don't see it bear fruit. That's why I started in March 2002 and our UEFA certification didn't come through until 2004. It took a long while but we have a really good programme that fits well for Iceland. I'm not saying it's perfect for Germany, Denmark or wherever, but it fits well for Iceland.'

He took UEFA's template and tailored it to Icelandic needs, mindful that the most talented players needed to be prepared for moves abroad. The result was a holistic approach. 'I always thought the most important thing was to reach the masses,' he says.

Coaches in north and east Iceland did not attend many courses in Reykjavík because to do so would require a domestic flight and overnight accommodation. In response, Eyjólfsson set off around Route 1 – the circuitous road that etches a tarmac ring around the island – and took the courses to the towns. UEFA courses are invitation only in other countries, but Eyjólfsson kept access open in Iceland.

Coaching qualifications soon became a status symbol. 'It exploded when we got the UEFA badges,' he explains. 'Everyone wanted the little ID that you can keep in your wallet to show people you were a UEFA-licensed coach. We found that was really encouraging.'

Change always faces some resistance. Gnarled coaches were sceptical. They pointed to their decades-in-the-dugout apprenticeship. What could a course teach that they had not already learned on the job? That attitude disintegrated as the new generation of coaches proved to be, actually, rather good – with innovative and thorough methods.

The KSÍ swerved resistance from clubs by brandishing a stick to accompany the carrot of better coaches for their young players. A club-licensing system made it mandatory for clubs to educate their coaches. If, for example, the champions of Iceland did not have a licensed coach in charge of their under-14 team, the first team would not be allowed to defend their title. The KSÍ relaxed the rule after the initial shock tactic had the desired effect, but clubs still receive a fine if their youth coaches do not have the required expertise.

Eyjólfsson benefited from being part of a small organisation. New policy did not meander through a bureaucratic labyrinth of associations, boards and committees. On several occasions he asked whether, after years of frozen prices, it was time to increase the cost of courses to reflect the inclusion of new books. The answer was always no. The KSÍ absorbed the cost. While Iceland's burgeoning financial sector chased profit in the mid-2000s, the KSÍ held steadfastly to the egalitarian principle that wealth should not incubate in a Reykjavík bank account but be reinvested through the clubs.

That conviction has not wavered despite the success of the national team swelling the KSÍ's coffers. Between 2016 and 2018, the KSÍ distributed about £8.5 million to Icelandic clubs, much of it revenue generated from the European Championship and the World Cup. That sum may seem trivial in the shadow of big-ticket transfer fees, but it is a significant injection of money in an ecosystem of amateur and semi-professional clubs.

The first Icelandic coaches passed the UEFA B course in early 2004. By 2018, 669 Icelanders held the UEFA B licence, 240 held the UEFA A, and, courtesy of a link with the English FA, 17 held the UEFA Pro Licence.

One non-Icelandic coach – who counts Iceland as one of 27 countries he has worked in – suspects that the KSÍ awards UEFA licences to coaches who do not meet the required standards in other countries. He may be right. The bar may be lower in Iceland, yet the scale of quality coaching is unparalleled.

There are no volunteer dads on the touchline, barking spittle-flecked orders at a son who is losing the will to live the dreams of his father. Icelandic children are marinated in football, and not in the twee way that we romanticise it in the United Kingdom: dads hoisting wide-eyed kids over turnstiles and into a thronging crowd. UEFA-licensed coaches train Icelandic children from the age of six.

What do all these coaches coach? The answer, more or less, is whatever they want. A rough syllabus exists, but with ample room for variation.

'The clubs decide how they coach their players from the age of six up to the first team,' Eyjólfsson says. 'But there are certain guidelines. You have to teach them technical skills. Which technical skills are most important? That's up to you.'

The KSÍ offers a framework without being dogmatic. There are two reasons for this compromise. The first rests upon a phrase Eyjólfsson heard as a young coach: 'If you have the same recipe, you will always bake the same cake.' A fully centralised process will create homogenous players. Eyjólfsson expands: 'You don't want to coach everyone the same way because you want different types of players who can play different systems. There needs to be a degree of freedom in coach education. That's why coaches don't have to do their refresher courses with the KSÍ. They can go abroad, observe training at a football club and talk to their coaches.'

Over a tar-thick coffee, Arnar Bill Gunnarsson – who took over from Eyjólfsson as the technical director at the KSÍ in 2013 – explains that scarcity is the second reason for devolving power to individual clubs and coaches. Iceland has too few players to create replicas.

'We believe coaches are independent,' he says. 'We don't tell the coaches to all do the same thing because we have so few players. The under-17s, for example, may want to play like the national team – which usually plays 4-4-2 – but the under-17s may not have two good strikers. So we keep it open. It's down to each coach.'

Arnar Bill shares Eyjólfsson's belief in the importance of coherent long-term thinking. He has tweaked certain things, but principles like ability-based grouping – splitting children into A, B and C teams to ensure they play equal opposition – remain entrenched.

The fundamental principle is to engage children early, to sow the seeds of a passion that will breed perseverance. Overt technical coaching comes later, as does specialisation. The KSÍ encourages children to practise other sports, like handball, basketball or athletics, alongside football until the age of 13 or 14. Aron Gunnarsson played handball for Þór Akureyri when he was 15 and still holds the record for the youngest goalscorer in the Icelandic First Division. No wonder he can land a throw-in on the penalty spot.

'We teach coaches that, for the first couple of years, football just has to be fun,' Eyjólfsson says. 'Don't take yourself too seriously as a coach. You can horse around with the kids and try to make it fun so they look forward to the next training. Don't think about results. Just let everybody play. Be encouraging and positive. Engage the parents. And you're successful if you increase the number of kids at the end of the year. If you can treat that inner motivation in the kids and make them interested and wanting to come to football, you've done your job.'

Coaches seek to capture the children's imagination with deceptively informal drills. Children at one club warm up with the Indiana Jones game, where they dribble around using only their heels. They are encouraged to imagine. Yet coaches often prefer the short, simple pass to the decadent flick or weaving run that have a higher chance of conceding possession. I ask Arnar Bill if hothousing young players in a sterile, UEFA-stamped environment may squeeze out their spontaneity and enthusiasm.

'No, I would say it's the complete opposite,' he responds. 'Inside the structured session you get a lot of freedom. The key for me is that if you go to a fun, well-structured session, you're more likely to fall in love with the game. And if you fall in love with the game, you'll play football outside the organised training sessions.

'Nobody becomes a really good player if they just show up three times a week for training. You have to stay out on the pitch for fun. I believe more players will do that if they have quality sessions when they start playing. The coaches who have the youngest players are absolutely vital.' As if on cue, he breaks off to speak to a coach who will be sitting his UEFA A exam that afternoon.

Though the KSÍ prioritises participation and spontaneity, youngsters have access to a busy calendar of competitive football in the form of league competitions and summer tournaments that draw hordes of players and parents from across the country. Geir Þorsteinsson – the former president of the KSÍ – believes the frequency of matches is crucial. 'Nobody likes to only train,' he says. 'You will not keep children in the game if they are not competing.' In previous decades only one team could represent a club at each age group, meaning dozens of children trained during the week with no promise of a match at the weekend. Now, a club may arrive at an under-11 tournament with five or six teams.

Geir recalls that in the early 1980s, the KSÍ reduced under-11 and under-12 football to seven-a-side and played on smaller pitches. This was an early conversion to small-sided games that have since become a staple of youth football. The principle remains the same in Iceland. Children incrementally progress from five-a-side to 11-a-side at a pace that encourages technical development and the ability to play in tight spaces rather than raw, biggest-in-the-class physicality.

If we had a time-lapse video of the days and weeks and months and years of work that produce a world-class footballer, it would show kick-ups, passing against a wall, bamboozling cones with silk-clad touches. Lots of mundane actions that accumulate.

Children can learn ball skills, but a willingness to accept that football is an exercise in delayed gratification is harder to impart. Paradoxically, early-stage coaches in Iceland use a missionary's mindset to inspire players to coach themselves.

To this end, the KSÍ distributed 16,000 'technical skills' DVDs to all registered players in Iceland aged 16 and under. The DVD contained 100 skills and drills that a young player could do on their own or with friends, in the garden or on a mini-pitch. But it needed to be something they would cherish, not like the other boxes gathering dust behind the PlayStation. So the men's and women's national team players got involved. They returned to their home towns to personally distribute DVDs to the children who idolised them. They were prepped to deliver the message that relentless training for a sustained period was the key to their success.

No amount of coaching DVDs, however, can remove the conflict at the heart of youth development: coaches must simultaneously think about the present and the future. The same questions nibble at every youth coach. Should I select an early developer because he is good today or should I select a late developer because he will be good in five years? Could I play an early developer alongside a late developer in midfield, to provide physical cover? There are no correct answers.

We are familiar with the Lilliputian spectacle of youth football. A brawny and bearded teenager marauds through a swarm of children who, though the same age, are yet to reach the promised land of puberty. Some 15-year-olds have the biological age of a 12-year-old, while others are biologically 18. Teenagers experience rapid physical and emotional change, yet adroit coaches must still assess their progress and potential.

It is easier for coaches to think about the present. Youth coaches often aspire to become assistants or head coaches at the senior level, where pay and prestige are higher. The best way to break into the old boys' club of first-team football is to win matches at youth level, but that places team results above individual development. Johan Cruyff identified a solution to this problem decades ago. One of his ideas was to rotate coaches around a club so that a first-team coach could take charge of the under-tens for a week. Unsurprisingly, it never caught on. It goes against the entrenched pattern of career progression.

Þorlákur Árnason was the head of youth coaching at the KSÍ until December 2018. He used LinkedIn as a platform to consider this conflict in a series of short essays.

'Most of the players in under-17 national teams all over the world are early developers,' he wrote in 2017. 'They are born early in the year. Their height and weight is above average.'

Þorlákur believes there is a problem with the measurement of success at youth level. 'Maybe we should start by calling the coach a "teacher of football". In youth football, results should not matter. You should measure the work of the coach on his progress with the group technically and tactically, not on results.'

The problem, of course, is that technical and tactical progress is difficult to quantify. Nevertheless, it is reassuring that those in charge of youth development in Iceland are critically engaging with such quandaries. The KSÍ is mindful that the need to focus on tomorrow is greater in Iceland than elsewhere. For every talented 15-year-old released by a German club, there is another wonderkid to replace him. Iceland does not have that luxury. Iceland cannot afford to lose players because there are so few. That is why Icelandic players can play for their club – and receive UEFA-stamped coaching – until the age of 19. Nobody is rejected. And all players receive the same coaching until they are 15 or 16. Only then do the better players start to command extra attention.

Some players are so precocious that their path to professional football is clear by their tenth birthday, but most take longer to blossom. Alfreð Finnbogason scored Iceland's goal against Argentina at the World Cup. At 18 he was languishing in the Third Division at Breiðablik's feeder club, unable to cross the ravine that divides youth and senior football. Hannes Halldórsson, the goalkeeper who saved Lionel Messi's penalty, was rejected by a Third Division club in Iceland when he was 23 and did not turn professional until 29.

Youngsters like Alfreð and Hannes developed at a different pace to others. Some literature refers to their type as 'talent that whispers'. Not all talent announces itself with a bugle horn and a prancing statement read from a papyrus scroll. Iceland caters for the persistent late developers who would have been long discarded elsewhere.

Yet, despite all their impressive work to inspire and develop as many young players as possible, the KSÍ cannot cover every last detail.

'We teach some mental training,' says Arnar Bill. 'But it's very shallow. We only cover the tip of the iceberg because we don't have the hours. The course would be too big if we were to make everybody an expert in every area. It's down to the coach to specialise himself.'

How are individual coaches developing footballers above the shoulders? Part of the process of discovery involved a descent into the dingy six-kilometre tunnel that burrows beneath Hvalfjörður ('whale fjord'). The light at the end of the tunnel is Akranes, a sedate fishing town that was the heartland of Icelandic football long before mentality appeared in coaching manuals.

Twelve miles north of Reykjavík, Akranes is home to 7,000 people. A derelict factory dominates the harbour like a brutalist ghost from a prosperous past. Fishing boats no longer chug in and out with the same frequency as in 1956, when England's amateur team played Iceland in the first ever fixture between the two nations. Eight of the

Iceland team – nine according to some reports – were from Akranes.

The town's biggest club, ÍA, dominated Icelandic football for large swathes of the 20th century, producing a succession of professional players for export in the process. They have been less successful since the turn of the millennium, yet they remain the most decorated club in the country.

The view from the club's boardroom compensates for the ugly pebbledash floor. Soot-black boulders separate the stadium from the moody sea like protective lumps of coal. Pennants hang on the wall as triangular reminders of yesterday's successes. Barcelona, Feyenoord and Aberdeen all visited to brace an onshore wind that slices across the pitch like a scythe.

Lúðvík Gunnarsson was a ballboy when Akranes beat Feyenoord 1-0 in 1993. Now he is the head of youth at ÍA and he wants youth development to mean more than technique and tactics and fitness.

'For me as a coach,' he says, 'developing the players as people is one of my main goals. I have to work with my coaches to help the kids develop mentally.

'I think we train football too much,' he continues. 'Maybe we should put together a curriculum on how to help them mentally. Only the strong ones will survive in professional football, so what are we doing there? We started with mentors.'

Every fortnight he meets one-on-one with teenage players he has seen rise through the age groups. They talk about football and on-pitch development, but other questions are more important: how are you feeling? Is everything going well at school? Are you still seeing that girl? The travails of adolescence. They embrace it even when the talking gets tough, Lúðvík claims.

'I'm very upfront. I do the real talk. I had one guy who now plays in Sweden. I trained him when he was younger. I knew him quite well. He was injured for two years and played no football. It was difficult for him to come back. He was a little bit arrogant but for me, it was just insecurity. I told him, "People think you're rude because of how you act and how you talk to them." He was quite surprised. I said, "I think it's because you're insecure. You need to loosen up a little and enjoy life more." You can't just say the beautiful things. You have to say the things they need to hear.'

Several players from Akranes have represented Iceland at youth level since Lúðvík and his colleagues introduced the mentoring programme. Arnór Sigurðsson is the flagship export, having joined CSKA Moscow in 2018 and played in the Champions League while still a teenager. Meanwhile, the ÍA under-19 side triumphed in their domestic competition to qualify for the 2019/20 edition of the prestigious UEFA Youth League. The youngsters from Akranes recorded a blistering 16-1 aggregate victory over FC Levadia of Estonia, but were eliminated by a strong Derby County team that went on to beat Borussia Dortmund in the following round.

Mentoring may not be groundbreaking, and nor does correlation imply causation. Yet there is a sense within the club that investing in the players as people is not only the responsible thing to do but that it also improves performance. Football is, fundamentally, a people business after all.

'Mentality is more likely to get you somewhere than just your ability to play football. I know some guys who suck at football. Honestly. Anyone could do what they do. But they're such good characters that they get contracts with Icelandic Premier League clubs. So it is important.'

Yet Lúðvík also appreciates his responsibility to the vast majority of players who will not progress to the professional game and have no desire to pursue that path. This is easier for semi-professional outfits in Iceland than player-production factories affiliated to big clubs elsewhere in Europe, where little Jonny becomes a commodity as soon as he can tie the laces on his boots. Unlike professional academies, ÍA does not exist solely to produce footballers. The club is woven into the fabric of the local community. Its function is to develop well-rounded people as much as to polish a new left-back for the first team.

We leave the charcoal views in the boardroom as Lúðvík leads me to the indoor football house adjacent to the stadium. A 12-year-old boy with blonde hair and skittish energy thuds a ball against the concrete base of the wall, alternating between right foot and left. He is the youngest son of Joey Guðjónsson, the ÍA manager and former Burnley and Real Betis midfielder.

'He'll make it,' Lúðvík says sagely. 'He's always in here.'

The under-19s are doing a possession drill. One team pings the ball to feet as their fluorescent-bibbed opponents try to thwart the tiki-taka. Lúðvík points out a languid player who wears a green headband to shield his ears from the chill. We stand, arms crossed, as he glides from space to space, omnipresent, as if time moves more slowly for him than his team-mates. He recently spent time on trial at Ajax.

Lúðvík treats the mental development of youth players like a Rubik's cube: something to tweak until he intuits an effective combination for each individual. Sometimes he stays silent on the touchline for an entire match. He wants his players to learn to resolve problems themselves on the pitch. For a few parents, the coach is not coaching unless he is shouting. But most trust Lúðvík to innovate.

'I'm looking forward to the next time a player gets pissed off on the pitch,' he says with a grin. 'Have you noticed the top-level coaches passing instructions to their players on bits of paper? When a player next gets frustrated, I'm going to pass him a bit of paper, folded up. It will just have a smiley face on it. I want to see how he reacts.'

The football industry is prone to forget that children are not mini-adults. Lúðvík personifies a shift away from authoritarian, hairdryer-treatment coaching, towards a style based on empathy and emotional intelligence. This is not exclusive to Icelandic coaches, but they are in the vanguard.

Oliver Sigurjónsson, too, is a proponent of this movement. When he fell out of love with playing football, he fell in love with coaching it.

Oliver is approaching his 23rd birthday when we meet in Bodø, Norway, where he plays for Bodø/Glimt. Although he has two Iceland caps, his stock as a player peaked seven years earlier. He was training with the first team at Breiðablik – 500m from the family home – by the time he was 15. He attracted interest from abroad. Lazio made an offer and he spent a period on trial at AC Milan. Yet, by the age of 19, Oliver was back in Iceland after a frustrating three-year stint at AGF in Denmark. He was back at Breiðablik, the club with a blazing torch on its badge, with his internal fire for football flickering.

'I expected to be in the first team more in Denmark,' he says, his stubble bristling on the collar of a black puffer jacket. 'I didn't get the playing time and I didn't train as often as I wanted. I also broke up with my girlfriend, who I had been with for four years. There were a lot of bad things in one soup. I went back to Iceland with a bad feeling about being a professional footballer.'

Like the players who did not make the breakthrough at Norwich, Oliver was another young Icelander left deflated by a challenging experience in a foreign academy. The volume of young players seeking a professional contract means this is a common occurrence, though it rarely spells the end of the dream. There is always another route to a professional career, even if it requires a step back in order to take two steps forward.

'There were a lot of effects on my confidence. I could have been like, "Fuck this, I'm quitting," but I'm not like that as a person.'

Oliver is comfortable being different. For one thing, he is the only Icelander I have met who does not drink coffee. And he dealt with rejection in a different way to most.

He first helped out with coaching at Breiðablik when he was 13. He shadowed his own coach during sessions with the under-tens and under-11s. Oliver enjoyed the challenge with a whistle between his lips and a set of cones under his arm.

So, when he returned from Denmark, he completed a UEFA B course funded by Breiðablik. His first position was assistant coach with the under-14s, before moving on to coaching specific skills to the best players at under-16 level – shielding the ball, one-on-one situations in defence and attack, and so on. Oliver was rejuvenated and coaching was part of that.

'I get really motivated when people doubt me,' he snarls. 'I just love it when people doubt me. I'm like, "I'm gonna fucking show them I'm good enough!" I took the coaching course because I wanted to become a better player by becoming a better coach. I want to have a better understanding of the game. I want to know what coaches are looking for. I want to know what scouts are looking for. I thought that if I could coach others, I could be a better coach of myself.'

Has it worked? 'Yes. I'm a tactical player. I read the game rather than go into tackles all the time. I want to see the game one step ahead, read it defensively. In training I think about things that other players maybe don't think about. I think about my position and why I might not be available to get the ball when another guy gets it.'

Coaching is one pillar of a supportive framework that Oliver has built around his football career. He also enrolled on a psychology module at the University of Reykjavík.

'You have to be good with personalities,' he responds when I raise my eyebrows. 'With some people you need to be really hardcore and with others you have to be really soft. That's something I struggle with as a person in the team and as a captain, like I was with the Iceland under-21s. Who am I approaching this way and who am I approaching that way?'

A personal training course followed. 'I've had a bit of a problem with injuries,' he elaborates. 'If I have information that can help me, I can use it on myself. It's my own body and my own career.'

I am taken aback by his unquenchable thirst for knowledge that will help him as a footballer and beyond into retirement. Oliver, however, is hesitant.

'Sometimes when you have a Plan B, you don't go after Plan A as much as you would if you only had Plan A. That's something I'm struggling with now.'

It is not as if his Plan B is opening a bar or a fashion label, I point out.

'That's true. But I'm always thinking about Plan A through Plan B.'

Although Oliver saw coaching as a means to improve himself as a player, it cultivated a passion for drawing the best from others. 'I love to teach people who want to be taught. I have my opinions on football and I really want to play my own style when I become a coach. I want to play the ball.'

Pep Guardiola and Jürgen Klopp are natural role models, as curators of the aggressive, technical brands of football Oliver favours. Julian Nagelsmann – the gilet-clad German who took Hoffenheim from the brink of relegation to the Champions League before joining RB Leipzig – has also made an impression.

'He has an iPad and a big screen at the training ground,' Oliver purrs, 'so he can show the players what they are doing right and wrong. I love that. It's like porn for coaches! You can give the players information in a concrete and quick method, so they stay focused and can learn more in a short space of time, because we don't have so many Einsteins in football!'

He also has clear views on youth development, which is the area of coaching that garners his interest. During his own youth career he encountered some coaches who prioritised winning, and others who placed technical and tactical development above results. Oliver situates himself towards the development end of the spectrum. This is based on a belief in exposing children to challenging situations early, while providing the support to help them learn from the experience.

'If I'm developing a guy who could play in a big league, he cannot experience mistakes, playing out from the back, or playing under pressure in a small area [for the first time] when he's 20. He should have been doing that his whole career.'

But his commitment to short passing is not sacrosanct. The needs of the individual come first. 'It's about what type of players you have and what you are developing as a coach. If I had a big target man who was really good, I would sometimes play a long ball, even though I want to play short, just to improve him as a player. If Kolbeinn Sigþórsson [Iceland's star striker] had never been played a high ball, he wouldn't now win 19 headers out of 20. As a youth coach you have to adapt to make the best players for the senior team, teams abroad, the youth national team, and so on.'

I had spoken to Oliver during my visit to the Nordlandshallen in Bodø simply because he happened to be an Icelandic player based there. I had not expected him to be one of the most erudite individuals I would speak to in the course of my time in Iceland. Indeed, I had judged the book by the cover. Oliver is a professional footballer and has modelled for fashion company Jack and Jones in Iceland; the chances of him completing a full house by being engaging and articulate seemed slim.

When Siggi Eyjólfsson sat in his modest meeting room in 2002, he knew that coaching in Iceland would not change with an overnight revolution. Rather, it would change as a result of a succession of sensible decisions made over months and years and decades. Taking courses to each corner of the country was one such decision. The training DVDs was another. It happened incrementally as a long-term vision took shape. Conscious, creative coaches like Lúðvík and Oliver personify that vision. And there are many more like them.

There are disputes and imperfections in Iceland like anywhere else. Influential voices like Heimir Hallgrímsson and Þorgrímur Þráinsson have expressed concern that the next crop of Icelandic players will not reach the level of the current golden generation, despite their access to phenomenal facilities and coaching. Indeed, there is a far-fetched suspicion that budding footballers now have it too easy in Iceland.

Coaches like Siggi, and those who have followed him at the KSÍ, are patient with their methods. To them, the next 20 years is more important than the next two, and they have created a model for youth development that will endure in the long term.

As Icelandic coaches pithily repeat, 'nowhere else in the world can children play football for as long, with as well-educated coaches, in as good facilities'.

Rúnar Geirmundsson

Heimir Hallgrímsson

# Chapter Nine
# Lars and Heimir

IF YOU say the words 'Lars' or 'Heimir' in Iceland, at any time and in any place, nobody will ask for a surname. The weight of their contribution to Icelandic football means no elaboration is necessary.

Lars Lagerbäck was appointed as the coach of the Iceland national team in October 2011. Thin-rimmed spectacles frame eyes that have seen it all in international football. He has brooded in the dugout at four European Championships – more than any other coach – and three World Cups. The austere tactician coached Sweden and Nigeria before Iceland, and Norway after.

Heimir Hallgrímsson joined Lars as assistant coach. He made his name at ÍBV, an Icelandic club limited by their isolation on Vestmannaeyjar. Yet, under Heimir's direction, ÍBV rose from Second Division cloggers to First Division title challengers. His reward was an opportunity to learn from an old hand.

Lars started as the master; Heimir was his pupil. That was the actual dynamic the first time they met.

Lars delivered a seminar to a group of candidates on the UEFA Pro Licence course. His future colleague was on the other side of the lectern. Heimir served a three-year apprenticeship as assistant coach. In 2014, they became joint-managers of Iceland. Then, after Lars left in 2016, Heimir took sole charge for a further two years.

Lars and Heimir might have been at different stages of their careers, but their routes to the top were both bound by unorthodoxy. I spoke to each of them separately within the space of a few weeks, ahead of the 2018 World Cup.

The American financial journalist Michael Lewis travelled to Iceland in 2009 to write an article for *Vanity Fair* about the global fiscal crisis. It was titled 'Wall Street on the Tundra'. Lewis combined investigative reporting with caustic observations that hovered between crude and outright offensive. He cast Icelanders as 'mousy-haired and lumpy' before declaring them 'among the most inbred human beings on earth'. One of Lewis's insults, however, struck a chord: 'The Icelandic male had a propensity to try to fix something it wasn't his job to fix.'

Heimir is in the foyer of the KSÍ's office at Laugardalsvöllur. He holds the disembodied arms of a plastic mannequin. The armless figure stares out of the window to the car park, the sleeves of its Iceland shirt hanging limply. The arms came off when we shifted the mannequin so that Heimir could have his photo taken alongside it. Now he takes it upon himself to repair the damage.

'You roll the sleeves up,' he instructs, while slotting each arm back into joint. I oblige, aware of the slapstick surrealism of the situation. It is a fiddly business. Once the surgery is complete, Heimir's eyes flash fondness up and down the mannequin in brief recognition of a job well done.

Few national team coaches would have bothered to fix it. Indeed, in many countries, Heimir would have no business fixing the national team. He is, famously, a dentist. His profession underpins the romance of the Iceland story. It fits and inflates the narrative of an ultimate underdog who rattles the elite with a team of tinkers and tailors and soldiers and sailors. In the news conference before Iceland's World Cup debut against Argentina, Heimir cut to the chase. 'Before anyone asks,' he said to the gathered media, 'I'm still a dentist and I will never stop being a dentist.'

Today, we settle in a suite overlooking the pitch. It is a Tuesday morning in April and that match against Argentina is two months away. The grass is easing from yellow to green. It is difficult to imagine a match being played here. It is too tranquil. On the other side of the athletics track, a Coca-Cola-emblazoned scoreboard loiters behind the goal on a tower of peeling concrete. It would feel vaguely Soviet were it not for the rampant advertising and the fjord on the horizon.

Heimir was not destined for dentistry. He was a teenager on Vestmannaeyjar who had to choose a subject to study at university on the mainland. His choice was computer science until the textbooks arrived. They contained pages and pages of dry mathematics. He reconsidered and followed the lead of his friend, who had opted for dentistry.

Heimir's attitude to education helps explain his willingness to change subject. To him, it is not just about the vocation.

'Education always improves you,' he says. 'It doesn't matter if it's 100 per cent connected to what you do. Education is always beneficial. Whatever subject you're doing at university, you will always gain from it because you will always be interacting with different kinds of people.

'That's the beauty of today,' he continues. 'Those who want to learn can learn so much. It's the same for coaches and players. They can access everything about nutrition or psychology, and study it 24/7. You can access what you want online and improve yourself every day. Or you can watch porn,' he adds with an avuncular grin.

Although Heimir kept the dentistry to himself on the UEFA Pro Licence course, it was never a barrier to coaching. Quite the opposite. Heimir values emotional intelligence and views players as people before athletes. Dentistry, like any medical profession, both demands and nurtures empathy.

'Every patient who comes to your dental chair is different,' he says. 'Some are afraid. Others are relaxed. When you have a new client you have to adapt to their personality, whether that's calming them down or whatever. Then you have to do something different when the next client comes in. It's the same with football players. To have 25 years' experience of dealing with clients one-on-one benefits me when it comes to talking to the players and owners and CEOs.

'The health of your personality comes down to how you react and relate to people who are different to you. If you can adapt and talk to all kinds of people, that shows a healthy personality.'

An education outside football's incestuous carousel of ideas encouraged Heimir to trust technology and data, as well as the game's received wisdom. Like former Arsenal coach Arsène Wenger, who studied politics and economics at the University of Strasbourg, Heimir was open to external influence.

'I started off really early with computers,' he says, kicking off the slippers he wears around the office. 'I have a big database of what I've done and what I've seen. I take videos of training, drills or whatever, clip the best bits and put them in the "organiser". If I do something for a meeting, I always file it so I can access it later. I don't like to do things twice. I like to spend a little more time doing it well the first time.'

Heimir returned to Vestmannaeyjar after university and opened his own clinic. Every so often he tells the secretary to make him available for appointments with long-term clients. It keeps his mind and fingers dextrous. Some coaches play golf to unwind; others uncork another bottle.

Heimir whips out wisdom teeth. But coaching was always his passion. He started at 17, tired of waiting for the elusive growth spurt that might have prolonged his playing career. Crucially, he had a mentor.

'There was a Polish coach there [Vestmannaeyjar] at the time – Grzegorz. A really intelligent, clever guy. He had a different way of thinking about football. It was all about the individual. He didn't mind if we lost the game, but he wanted every player to have a task that was suited to his standard. Maybe the team lost, but the players gained. The tasks were necessary for them to develop. It was a way of coaching that we hadn't seen before. I fell in love with coaching at that time.'

The young footballers of Vestmannaeyjar benefited from Heimir's infatuation. He coached several age groups during a 15-year period. His routine was regular: in the clinic from eight o'clock until three o'clock, home for a couple of hours, and then down to the club to coach. Heimir coached the ÍBV women's team for several years in the 2000s before taking charge of the men. Only when Heimir joined the Iceland set-up in 2011 did he consider coaching as a career. In Iceland, a dentist earns four or five times more than a coach of a First Division side. Even when he joined the national team, his mother questioned the sagacity of swapping security for the churn of football.

'I think it's special that a national team coach has also been a youth coach and a women's coach,' he smiles. 'I wasn't a professional player, so for me it was about going step by step, increasing my knowledge and responsibilities. It was the only way for me to progress to where I am today.'

That passion for youth development remains. The week after Iceland were eliminated from the World Cup, under-ten teams from across the country convened on Vestmannaeyjar for an annual tournament. Everyone wanted a photo with one of the rain-soaked referees. It was Heimir. Professional players are easy to manage compared to a kerfuffle of hyperactive ten-year-olds.

Now with Al-Arabi in the Qatar Stars League, Heimir is keen to savour the experience of professional coaching. Perhaps he appreciates his fortune more because he transitioned from 'civilian' life to professional football at a relatively late stage. Before we began the interview he had taken a picture of us on his phone. 'I do it with everyone who interviews me,' he explained.

Self-awareness should not be mistaken for a lack of self-belief. Heimir thought he was ready to be the sole coach of the national team in 2011, but the KSÍ had another man in mind.

Lars Lagerbäck remembers the first time he watched television. It was the semi-final of the 1958 World Cup. Sweden, the hosts, beat West Germany to secure a place in the final against Brazil and a 17-year-old prodigy by the name of Pelé. Lars was approaching his tenth birthday when he travelled to Stockholm to watch the match at a relative's house.

'It was just incredible to watch TV,' he recalls. 'You youngsters probably can't imagine growing up without that!'

Brazil beat Sweden in the final, but the tournament was formative for the young boy from the north.

Lars spent his childhood on a farm in the Medelpad province of Sweden, where tangled woodland covers the landscape like a thick-shag carpet. His father worked in the woods, deciding where and when the trees would come down. Translated literally from Swedish, his job title was 'forest inspector'. Lars was often out with his father and he learned from a young age to get out and get involved.

Six decades after Lars was transfixed by 22 pixelated protagonists on the television screen, he is in more urban surroundings. The Ullevaal Stadion is home to the Norway national team. Lars became their coach in 2017. The stadium rises from the Oslo suburbs, a mass of black glass joined at the hip to a retail centre. There can't be many places where a football fan can collect their match ticket and buy an open-water canoe at the same time.

Lars speaks slowly and deliberately. He divides his gaze between the television cameras and the notepad on the table. It is the press conference to announce the Norway squad for matches against Iceland and Panama. Lars carries an easy authority as he moves to the back of the room to speak individually to journalists.

Once the Norwegian press-pack has dispersed, we go upstairs to a meeting room overlooking the pitch. He smiles more freely away from the crowd, when his audience consists solely of a distant groundsman and me. He pulls a frothing coffee from the machine and thinks back to military service, his first step after school.

'In the army you learn discipline,' he says. 'The boss is the boss, and things like that. You learn to function in a group and take orders. In a way I think it's a good education, even if some things are bad, ridiculous even. There were officers who forced you to do things that were totally silly, just to show their power. If I could choose a world I would prefer to have no armies at all.'

Apart from the draconian leadership, Lars did not find the experience challenging – he was used to being outside in the Swedish winters – but it helped form his conviction that discipline is necessary for good team spirit.

A degree in political science and economics – a similar academic strand to Wenger – followed military service, but neither Marx nor Plato could shift his attention away from football. Between his studies, Lars turned out for Gimonäs CK, a now-defunct team in the amateur leagues. Perhaps it would be more accurate to say he studied between the gaps in football.

Lars soon realised that he would progress further off the pitch than on it, and he took on an administrative role in charge of the youth divisions at the club. That led to his break at the prestigious Swedish School of Sport and Health Sciences.

Lars was one of five students on the football coaching course, which was partly run by the Swedish FA. So many success stories begin with a chance encounter. This one is no different. One of the other students introduced Lars to Bob Houghton, who would shape how Lars thought about football.

Houghton's managerial career began in the depths of English non-league. He started at Hastings United and progressed to Maidstone United, neither of which were illustrious names in the game. Then, in 1974, he made the leap to Malmö. Houghton was only 27 when he took the job. Five years later, he made Malmö the first and only Swedish club to reach the European Cup Final, where they lost to Brian Clough's Nottingham Forest.

'Bob is one of my absolute best friends,' Lars says. 'I was down at Malmö very often. He brought something totally new to Swedish football. He was the first coach in Sweden, I would say, who worked 100 per cent on organising a team.

'He changed the general tradition of training in Sweden. We had a long pre-season with a lot of physical work. But Bob kept the players on the pitch. He worked on cooperation between the players. He had a big influence on my philosophy as a coach. He gave me a base, which is that to organise a team is the most important thing.'

Lars wedges a wad of tobacco between his cheek and gum and continues. 'If you look at football today, all the teams that are winning – clubs and national teams – have a clear way of playing. It's easy to analyse them. It could be very difficult to play that way, like when Barcelona and Pep had that possession football. But there were clear roles for the players. I got to know Pep a little bit and I visited him at Man City. He *really* organises his team.'

Armed with Houghton's innovative template, Lars moved swiftly through the coaching ranks. A youth coaching role at the Swedish FA led to leadership of Sweden B in the 1990s and the senior national team in the 2000s. Lars led his nation to the knockout stages of three consecutive tournaments: the World Cups in 2002 and 2006, with Euro 2004 between.

After a short spell in charge of Nigeria, retirement beckoned. Although the Super Eagles failed to qualify from their group at the 2010 World Cup, the Nigerian FA immediately offered Lars a four-year contract. He declined, unenthused by the prospect of spending his mid-sixties in a gated community.

Lars still owns the farm he grew up on in Medelpad, north Sweden. Spending time there is important to him. That is one reason why he declined lucrative offers to enter club football. But the itch of curiosity never goes away.

'I always like the challenge of seeing what you can do. That's one of the most interesting things with my job. What can you do with a group of people? And it's always fascinating to go to another country, learn something and develop as an individual.'

It was this fascination that led Lars to Iceland.

Iceland were languishing in 108th place in the FIFA rankings when Lars and Heimir arrived in Reykjavík. But they had good raw materials to work with. A chrysalis of promising players was emerging. Iceland under-21s had qualified for the European Championship in 2011 and, on the way to qualification for that tournament, the youngsters had slaughtered a Germany side captained by Mats Hummels by a score of 4-1. Most of the stars of that cohort – including Gylfi Sigurðsson, Jóhann Berg Guðmundsson and Aron Gunnarsson – already had senior international experience.

The task of fulfilling their potential fell to Lars and Heimir, who first had to define a clear working environment. It was as much a test of project management as football acumen. Having absorbed the methods of 'English Bob' Houghton and his close ally 'English Roy' Hodgson in the 1970s and 1980s, Lars refined his own approach and arrived in Iceland with a formula.

'We took away what was very common in football, and what still is: rules. We started to make guidelines instead – of how to live and work off the pitch and how we should play on the pitch. The basic thing for us was cooperation. What we wanted to do with our philosophy was get the players to understand why we win football games. As coaches we often educate players too little in why we win and perform well.'

Lars worked with his staff and the players to develop about 30 guidelines. They could be as small as 'no coffee during team meetings'. In a sense, the guidelines are a euphemism. If a player were to flaunt them, he would be out of the team. But while rules imply despotism, guidelines based on mutual agreements hand more responsibility to the players.

The subtle distinction became clear to me when Lars spoke off the record during the interview. I reached across the table to pause the Dictaphone.

Lars interrupted my movement. 'Can I trust you?'

'Of course.'

He gestured to leave the Dictaphone running.

'I just ask that you promise,' he said. 'Otherwise I'll be extremely disappointed.'

There was something about this exchange, the way he enunciated each syllable of 'disappointed', that cast a light on his man-management style and why the fabled guidelines form an integral part of his philosophy. He passes responsibility to the players and expects them to value that.

Mutually-agreed guidelines create a circle of trust that empowers the group.

Heimir explains what the formula means to him: 'Lars had a formula he had been using in Sweden for 20 years. He's probably the longest-serving national coach in the world. So he brought this formula and we reviewed it, we talked to the players about it in meeting after meeting, then we implemented it.

'Slowly and steadily we built a working environment that we all accepted. It was totally different from what I heard was here before – real disorganisation. Now there's total organisation about everything: how we should train, how we should play, how we should behave, how we should dress, how we should live together. Everything.'

Lars emphasises that this is not a one-way conversation. Players have the opportunity to present feedback and suggest alterations.

'I hope I'm not too fundamentalist,' he says. 'I think many coaches work like dictators. They have very little dialogue with the players. With the guidelines and the way we work on the pitch, I try to get the players to understand why we do what we do.'

Although there is room for discretion, Lars will not change his fundamental principles. 'The method, the way of working, I will not change. That's why I've chosen to say "No thank you" to big money. I want to work where I know I can work how I want to. Of course, you have to adapt though.'

In Iceland, adaptation meant embracing the locals' independence. 'If something needs to be done they do it themselves,' Lars says. 'I can tell you a story as I'll probably never write my memoirs. In the first meeting I had with the staff – and I only had Icelandic staff – we spent two days sitting together, going through how I wanted to work.

'On the second day, one of the guys got up and left. I thought he'd gone to the toilet. But he didn't come back. I asked where he had gone. "I don't know," someone said. "He probably had something to do."'

Heimir acknowledges this streak in the Icelandic character. 'We adjusted [the formula] to the Icelandic way of thinking. Swedish and Icelandic people are similar in many ways. But we're still a bit different. Like with patience for meetings. Swedish people are used to having long meetings whereas we're a bit more individualistic. We fix things ourselves rather than having a long talk about it.'

What does the formula mean in practice? Icelandic players repeat two things when asked what it is like to work under Lars and Heimir: repetition and meetings. Endless meetings.

The two coaches admit that their methods can be mundane. 'If you ask one of the Icelandic players and you get an honest answer, they will say that they were really fed up with all the repetition and organisation,' Lars says. 'I mean, I would say about 90 per cent of training is about the organisation of the team. But that is why we had pretty good results with Sweden and Iceland. The players get to a high lowest level. Even if they have a bad day, they all know what to do and how to cooperate.'

'It's more or less only tactical training,' Heimir adds. 'There's nothing about fitness or technique. You can't improve a player's technique when you have two or three training sessions with them. It's more about trying to sync the team together.'

The daily meetings also worked to that end. Every international break begins with a welcome meeting, followed by separate meetings on attack, defence, tactics and the opposition. Lars and Heimir believe an emphasis on organisation is the most effective use of limited time. Whereas club coaches work with their team throughout the season, international duty is scattered across the calendar in blocks of six or seven days.

'Continuity is a big thing,' the Icelander says. 'You have to build on what you've been doing. You can't go from east to west. A sentence that Lars often said to me clings in my head: "Be ambitious but don't be overambitious." You have such limited time. You can't do everything. You have to be really selective with what you do, especially with new things you introduce, because it won't stick in the players' minds.'

Lars reiterates the importance of continuity and delivers apt political commentary in the process. 'I always say to people when I give presentations that the most negative word is "populism". If you want to be a leader you have to stay away from populism.' He believes a coach should never follow fleeting trends in football as that distracts from the best way to use the available players.

Heimir found this advice particularly valuable. He had not worked with professional players before 2011 and admits that he would have been swayed by those with elite experience.

'Eiður Guðjohnsen would have said, "This is how we do it at Barcelona," and I would probably have said, "Yeah! Let's do it like Barcelona." Then Kolbeinn Sigþórsson would have said, "This is how we do it at Ajax," and we would have changed everything from Barcelona to Ajax.'

The players responded well to the clarity provided by the formula. Grétar Steinsson remembers the first call he received from Lars. He was filling up his car with petrol in Bolton when a foreign number appeared on his phone. Grétar was disillusioned with international football at the time. The call changed his outlook.

'When someone is on your level and speaks the same language as you ... straight away after that call I was 100 per cent in.' His enthusiasm grew after the first international break under the new leadership. 'Even when we weren't winning, I still knew what the plan was. Win, lose or draw, this is what we do and we're going to do it well.'

Results did not come immediately, however. Iceland played four friendly matches in the first half of 2012 and lost all four, sliding to 131st in the FIFA rankings. But there were signs of improvement. Consecutive 3-2 defeats away to France and Sweden appear in a positive light when compared to a 4-0 thrashing at the hands of a limited Hungary side nine months earlier.

'Questions like, "Is it OK to do this now?" slowly just stopped,' Heimir says. 'Everyone knew what to do when they came to the national team. That is so necessary. The players are all different characters. They're used to playing and behaving in a certain way. When they come here, they have to know what's expected of them.'

The players knew their roles. So did Lars and Heimir. The Icelander focused more on the opposition, on defining their strengths and weaknesses. The Swede used that information to work with the team itself.

By the time the players arrive for international duty, all of the preparatory work is done. The tactics are confirmed, training sessions planned and video clips edited. The longest part of the process was to convince themselves of the best course of action.

'If we can't convince ourselves, we can't convince the players,' Heimir reasons.

Iceland were a team transformed by 2013. One match in September of that year was a declaration of intent. Switzerland led Iceland 4-1 in a World Cup qualifier. Thirty-five minutes of the match remained. The Swiss were strong. Especially at home. Yet Iceland scored three in the second half to level the match at four goals apiece. Jóhann Berg Guðmundsson scored a last-minute equaliser to complete his hat-trick. That night in Basel catalysed a push for the 2014 World Cup, which ended in play-off defeat to Croatia. Iceland had never been so close to a major tournament. The dream was not over, though; it was on hold.

Heimir became joint-manager after that disappointment. Over the next two years, Iceland flew through the qualifying campaign for Euro 2016, beating the Netherlands home and away in the process. They did so using Freddie Steele's 4-4-2, bound by fierce organisation. The defence moved forwards and back, left and right like the rigid figurines on a table football rod. Industrious midfielders stifled the opposition, and Gylfi Sigurðsson applied the sprinkle of stardust. The two strikers worked just as hard as the rest. They could create chances from speculative long balls in a way that a lone striker could not.

I ask Heimir if he ever thinks about aesthetics when forming a team. He bristles and chews on the question. Then comes the curt response: 'I could be a little offended because you're saying the football we play isn't nice. If we were to play like Spain we would always be a bad replica. We don't have those qualities, so why should we play that style? We should have our own identity and our own playing style. You play according to what you can do, not what you want to do.'

Football is a contest of goals, not aesthetics. The coach must be realistic. In Iceland's case, that means guerrilla tactics.

The correlation between possession and points is strong. *The Economist* analysed competitive matches between 2009 and 2017 and found that Iceland averaged 46.9 per cent of possession. This would typically equate to

1.1 points per game. Iceland, however, managed 1.5 points per game across the sample of 47 matches. The numbers from the 2018 World Cup qualifying campaign were starker still: Iceland converted a mere 41.6 per cent of possession into 2.2 points per match. No other team matched that efficiency.

It is possible that Iceland surfed a tidal wave of good fortune. Yet the more likely explanation is that Lars and Heimir found a way to create better chances than their opponents, while still playing defensive football.

'We adapt by attacking in different ways,' Heimir explains. 'We score one goal a game from set pieces. Some teams struggle to score one goal a game at all.' As for possession? 'We don't give a shit about that. Our identity is not about possession. It's not about having the best football players. We know that the individual technical ability of players in Iceland is not the same as in most other national teams. We adapt to that reality.'

Lars left after Euro 2016, leaving Heimir in sole charge. There were certain changes to tactics. Meetings became shorter. But the body of Lars's formula remained.

Some observers in Iceland credit Lars with making profound, pervasive changes. They present him as a missionary who introduced professionalism to a directionless rabble. Private jets are used as evidence to support this theory. Iceland generally travelled to away matches on commercial flights, often with stopovers in London or Amsterdam. The KSÍ began to charter private flights around the same time that Lars became coach. But correlation does not mean causation. Lars did not invent professionalism in Icelandic football; he raised it to a higher level. He is as much a symptom of professionalisation as a cause. The KSÍ had completed its wave of investment in facilities and coach education. That meant more money was available for chartered flights and, indeed, for expensive foreign coaches.

That said, Lars's influence as a symbolic figurehead was profound. Respect and legitimacy enabled him to implement his formula. Anyone seeking to make cultural changes needs both. The players would not have responded if a disrespectful foreign coach had arrived and looked down his nose. Lars did the opposite.

Lars and Heimir share an endearing trait: modesty. This was more evident than ever on 2 June 2018, the day Heimir's Iceland played Lars's Norway in a pre-World Cup friendly.

Heimir had a pre-match ritual. Before every home match he went to Ölver, a dingy sports bar in one of the less salubrious suburbs of Reykjavík. It is the watering hole of Tólfan, the rambunctious supporters' group formed in 2007 to improve the atmosphere at Iceland matches home and away. Heimir would give the supporters the team news before it was announced publicly.

When Heimir began the ritual in 2011, eight supporters were there to see it. Before the match against Norway Heimir arrived a couple of hours before kick-off, a laptop bag slung over his shoulder, to find 200 people crammed into the bar.

Heimir preached from a small stage, at the rear of which was a Harley-Davidson in a glass case – taxidermy for the Hell's Angels. He clicked from slide to slide on his presentation. A Nelson Mandela quotation featured:

'It always seems impossible until it's done.' Then came images of the Greece team that won Euro 2004 and the Denmark team that won Euro 1992. Then, finally, the line-up and tactics, explained with a flurry of red dots and arrows.

The beery crowd were dotingly engrossed until Heimir applied the final words to his final slide. In that moment there was a commotion at the side of the stage. People rose to their feet. Some climbed on chairs. Someone had made a subtle entrance through the fire exit. From my vantage point at the back of the bar I glimpsed a tracksuited figure with silvery hair: Lars. He had never accompanied Heimir to Ölver during his five-year spell in charge of Iceland; only when returning as the Norway coach did he step through the threshold.

'It's fantastic to be back again,' Lars said, a little overwhelmed. The occasion had penetrated his dour exterior. 'And I have a present for Tólfan.'

'I hope it's alcohol,' Heimir chirped.

'I think they can fix that for themselves,' Lars responded as he reached into a plastic bag and retrieved a Norway shirt.

'To Tólfan, good luck at the World Cup,' read the message on the front. I felt like I was witnessing an intimate ceremony that I had no business being part of, as if I were crashing a family wedding. A representative of Tólfan reciprocated with a commemorative ring.

Lars continued: 'Maybe me leaving was the best thing for Icelandic football, because Heimir has taken you to the World Cup. I hope we'll still be friends even if we beat you tonight.'

Heimir took over. He captured the essence of the moment. 'It's a unique moment: two national team coaches coming together to a pub before their teams play each other.'

Lars and Heimir appreciate the serendipity of the situation they walked into and give credit to the players. Few coaches would so readily admit that perhaps they were lucky to work with a certain group of players, rather than the other way around. As Heimir puts it to me:

> The good thing about this team, this group of guys, is that they genuinely like each other. They like to praise the guy next to them. They don't take the credit for themselves and that's so different to the world as it is today. You have people taking selfies and asking for praise because they've got a new shirt or new hair. That is the reality of today. It will be more and more about praise. People will think, 'I'm going to do something so I get praise.' In this group, it's the total opposite. They like to give their team-mates the spotlight and I think that's unique. Absolutely unique.

# Chapter Ten
# Golden boys

THERE IS an elusive magic to a generation of players who grow together. Perhaps that is why they are always described by the same adjective. They are always 'golden'.

We often look upon such generations with a fateful sense of what could have been. The English wince at the memory of the 2006 World Cup and a squad that weighed so much less than the sum of its parts. Then there are cases like the Class of '92 – Beckham, Giggs, the Neville brothers, Butt and Scholes – whom Sir Alex Ferguson plucked from Manchester United's academy at the same time. All stars in their own right, they are still identifiable by the collective.

The magic stems from the bond we perceive them to share. We, as football fans, relate to that. When we see a group of players who have grown together from boys to men, we do not see colleagues nor team-mates. Instead, we see a group of friends, like the groups we cherish; with in-jokes, ribbing and that unique energy when all gather around a table. We see a human connection that strips away the uniform image of the modern footballer, media-trained to say words that mean nothing while clutching a Louis Vuitton washbag.

Iceland has a 24-carat golden generation. Five of the team that bewildered England in 2016 had played together for the under-21s. Some had shared a pitch since they were 14.

Aron Gunnarsson is the captain and the core. He delivers the final words before the trill of the referee's bell summons the players to the tunnel. On the pitch he is the adhesive midfielder that binds the team, and the provider of trebuchet throw-ins, a residual weapon from a youth spent playing handball. He relies on graft as much as craft. Aron's commitment does not waver. He watched the birth of his first child from Kazakhstan, where Iceland played a European qualifier in 2015. When 'it's the final push' echoed through Skype and his son wailed for the first time, Aron was slumped in the corridor, speechless, tearful.

Alongside him in the centre of midfield is the star: Gylfi Sigurðsson. His value to the team comes not only from his gliding feints and devilish set-piece deliveries, but also his work ethic. In a scene from *Inside the Volcano* – the documentary that tracks Iceland's qualification campaign for Euro 2016 – Gylfi stands alone in the Amsterdam Arena 24 hours before Iceland face the Netherlands. There is a taut anticipation in the emptiness of the stadium. He places a ball on the edge of the box and arcs a free kick into the near corner. An echoed shout from off camera breaks the hypnotic repetition. 'Gylfi, the bus is going.' When the best player has a relentless work ethic, it lifts the rest of the team. If Gylfi can do it, what is their excuse?

Jóhann Berg Guðmundsson plays on the right of midfield. He and Gylfi have been close since they played together for Breiðablik as kids. When Jóhann Berg wasn't scratching around at Breiðablik's indoor hall, he was at Gylfi's house. He spent part of his childhood in London when his parents relocated for work. Spells at Fulham and Chelsea aided his development. They also instilled a mastery of the phrase 'to be fair', a tic that replaces punctuation in many post-match interviews.

On the left flank, Birkir Bjarnason scampers with brooding intensity, his blonde mane flowing behind him. He becomes acquainted with every blade of grass on his side of the pitch. His one-track mind was always in a groove. As a stringy ten-year-old in Akureyri, a town as harsh as its syllables, he would pretend not to hear when the coach called for him to be substituted. The strong-silent vibe remains on promotional posters for *66°North*, the Icelandic clothing company for whom he models.

In attack, Kolbeinn Sigþórsson was the most precocious of all. He toppled records as a ten-year-old with ostentatious poise in front of goal. It was clear then that he would play for Iceland. Real Madrid and Arsenal scouted the youngster from Reykjavík, the next Eiður Guðjohnsen. He spent a fortnight on trial at the North London club before moving to the Netherlands as a teenager. Injury ruled him out of the squad for the World Cup. Yet, despite barely playing between 2016 and 2018, he looks certain to surpass Eiður as Iceland's leading scorer.

Alfreð Finnbogason developed at a slower pace to the rest of them, but he was the scorer of Iceland's first-ever goal at a World Cup. A natural poacher, he scored 29 goals for Heerenveen in the Dutch Eredivisie in 2013/14. Only Cristiano Ronaldo, Luis Suárez and Jonathan Soriano scored more in the top European leagues. Equally as impressive as the goal haul itself, is that Alfreð could tell you about it in a polyglot mix of Icelandic, English, Dutch, Spanish, Italian and German.

These players were all born between 1988 and 1990. They formed the under-21 side that qualified for the European Championship in 2011. An Icelandic men's national team had never qualified for a major tournament. It was a significant milestone and an aperitif for what was to come.

The group graduated together to the senior team and became the nucleus of the side that reached the European Championship and the World Cup. Rúrik Gíslason also came from that under-21 cohort to represent Iceland in Russia. There are others, too, who have featured sporadically.

They are close friends. Several own summer houses next to each other in the Icelandic countryside. Jóhann Berg captures the camaraderie: 'We absolutely love meeting up. I've got six of my best mates here and I don't see them often. For us, it's just a joy to meet up and play with each other. There are no big egos. Everyone is on the same page and no one is bigger than the team.'

He believes the squad benefits from the wide diaspora of Icelandic players. Unlike players in the England squad, who almost exclusively play for Premier League clubs, the Icelanders do not compete against each other for titles one week then play together the next. There are no cliques that result from club alliance bleeding into the national set-up.

'We came in as winners,' Jóhann Berg says. 'We came in with a bit of ego, even though there were big players in the squad. We came in with a bit of arrogance, a bit of confidence. That's something you always want to have in a team.'

They have the right dosage of chutzpah. Gunnleifur Gunnleifsson was a gnarled goalkeeper when the youngsters bounded into the national team. Now 44, he is still the captain of Breiðablik.

'They were cocky,' he smiles, 'that's what they were. They were very self-confident from early on. But nice guys.'

Gunnleifur's greying temples bear the pockmarks of teenage tumult. Alcohol and drug addiction forced him to quit football at 17. Handball was his salvation. He got clean and played handball for Iceland at under-21 level, before returning to play with his feet. Those life experiences made him an important figure in the dressing room. He was not worried that the exuberant youngsters would cause friction, but rather that they would regress to the habitual mediocrity of the national team.

'I knew they were good players, but I was always afraid that they would adapt to us, the way we were, what we were doing with the national team. There was no special belief that we could do anything. We just went through the groups like, "Yeah, maybe we can take three points off the Faroe Islands here, one point there."'

Gunnleifur is happy to have been proved wrong. He chooses two matches against the Netherlands – the first in 2008 and the second in 2015 – to show the transformation in mentality.

'Seven years apart,' he says, leaving the words to hang. 'In the meeting in Rotterdam before the game in 2008, we just talked about trying to keep a clean sheet for the first 15 minutes, hanging on for the first 30 minutes, and let's see what that brings us. Before the Amsterdam game in 2015, the first thing that was said in the meeting was: "This is how we're going to beat the Netherlands." It went from black to white.'

Gunnleifur's disappointment at being omitted from the Iceland squad for Euro 2016 shows the strength of the bond within it.

'Everybody thought I was in,' he grimaces. 'So did I.'

His reaction was visceral. 'It's like a piece of my heart that I can't get back. I felt like I'd lost someone close to me. It was so hard. Some companies invited me to go to France to watch the games, but I couldn't. I wasn't ready.'

Did he feel bitterness? 'No,' he says resolutely. 'I love the guys and I was so happy for them, all of them.'

Aron forged the path from the under-21s to the senior team. He won his first cap at the age of 18 in 2008. Then, like the Pied Piper, he summoned the rest. Jóhann Berg and Rúrik followed six months later. Gylfi, Birkir, Alfreð and Kolbeinn made their debuts in 2010. There was no carefully laid plan for their transition. It happened because a desperate coach saw few alternatives.

Ólafur Jóhannesson sighs. 'What can I say? We were not a good team. Sometimes we won, sometimes we lost. We went up and down.'

Ólafur managed Iceland from 2007 until 2011. Now in his early sixties, he admires a panoramic view over the pitch at Valur – the ninth Icelandic club he has coached in a meandering career that began in 1980 in Vopnafjörður, an isolated town in the north-east corner of the country.

The Iceland job ought to have been the pinnacle of his career, but Ólafur soon realised that nothing had changed from the mediocrity that came before. His tenure began with defeats to Denmark, Belarus and Malta. The qualification campaign for the 2010 World Cup was sluggish: a patchwork Iceland side won once in eight matches, against Macedonia.

'I said to my assistant, "We're just doing the same as all the other coaches have done here. There's nothing going on." We had a good generation of young players. Very good young players. I said, "Let's take them in. It doesn't matter. Just let them play and they'll be good after five or six years. We have nothing to lose."'

It was a bold policy. Managers are judged on short-term results. Ólafur made himself vulnerable by prioritising the future.

'I thought nothing about myself,' he insists. 'We thought, what will happen? It's OK if it doesn't work, but [let's] take the chance because we have nothing to lose. I said to the players, "Maybe after five or six years you might go to the Euros or something like that." But actually, I didn't believe it at the time. Honestly, I didn't believe it.'

Failure brought no consequences. Mediocrity was acceptable because the KSÍ did not set expectations or targets. 'They just hired me as a coach,' Ólafur shrugs. 'We didn't talk much about what we should do or how we should do it. It was up to me.'

Paradoxically, that absence of expectation allowed Iceland's golden generation to bloom. It created an environment in which young players could acclimatise to international football without pressure. Iceland won one match in 2011 – 1-0 against Cyprus – but the 1988–90 generation were accumulating experience. By the time Lars Lagerbäck arrived in late 2011, most of them had around 20 caps each.

When the conversation turns to Lars, Ólafur's voice lilts with a sudden vulnerability, exacerbated by a sniffling cold that he dabs with a white handkerchief. 'It was the best thing that happened to Icelandic football when I left and they took on a professional trainer,' he says, his words laced with inferiority. 'Lagerbäck changed everything around the team.'

Ólafur's default setting is rueful self-deprecation when asked about his time with Iceland. It is his defence mechanism. He slips deeper into melancholy, as if our retracing the subject dredges up dark memories from his past. 'It is difficult for me to talk about it. I really don't want to talk about it ... about how it was. There were a lot of problems in the team when I took over. Sometimes when I wanted to go and watch players in Sweden and Norway, I was not allowed. There were a lot of problems here in Iceland.'

Concerns reached a peak in late 2010. Ólafur was forced to navigate a qualification match against Portugal without any of the 1988–90 youngsters – the spine of the team by that point – because the KSÍ decided they should drop down to the under-21s for a crucial two-legged play-off against Scotland. The under-21s won 2-1 home and away to secure a place at the European Championship the following summer. Viewed with hindsight, the value of tasting tournament football vindicates the KSÍ's decision. Yet that did not make the episode any less frustrating for Ólafur.

Ólafur admits that he should have foreseen the vast difference between club and international management. He tried to play attacking football but, with limited time on the training pitch, that desire created an imbalanced team. With experience only as a coach of semi-professional players, he lacked the legitimacy to enact institutional change.

'I tried to change a lot,' he says. 'But you have to have the board with you if you're going to change something, and they weren't ready to do that.'

Warmth returns to Ólafur's face as I steer the conversation back to the youthful players to whom he handed a chance. 'They know each other so well. They're the same age and they grew up together. They played against each other, and some were playing in the same team, since they were this high.' He lowers his palm to the carpet.

His prior gloom has faded. 'When you pick a squad, it's easier to work with them if they know each other. It was a great time, when I look back. They were a little bit wild!'

Ólafur watched the 1988–90 group when they were teenagers with their Icelandic clubs. He was particularly close to Gylfi, having played with his father in the 1970s and remained friends since. He recalls a summer when their families went on holiday together.

'Gylfi must have been ten or 11,' he says wistfully. 'His father said to me, "Óli, how much do you earn as a carpenter? Can you stop being a carpenter and train my son?"' He lets out a guffaw. 'I know him so well that I just laughed.'

Ólafur must be proud of his legacy, I probe, if not the results he achieved. He responds tentatively, as if self-praise is a tightly rationed commodity. 'Yes, I'm proud of it. I am proud of it, even though we weren't successful. Just to know the players, to go and play in big stadiums ... it was a great time. I learned a lot about myself and about football.'

A wide range of people I spoke to – from journalists to coaches to players – emphasised Ólafur's part in the most successful period in Icelandic football. He planted the seeds that germinated when Lars and Heimir took over. The one person who seems unconvinced is Ólafur himself.

Nowadays an individual operates behind the scenes in the Iceland set-up to make sure the players do not suffer the same fragile confidence. Þorgrímur Þráinsson's past is intertwined with Valur, the Reykjavík-based club that Ólafur led to consecutive league titles in 2017 and 2018. Þorgrímur captained Valur in the late 1980s, in the twilight of a football career that included 17 caps for Iceland. Now in his late fifties and with the assiduous grooming and chiselled cheekbones of Roger Moore's James Bond, Þorgrímur is the president of Valur.

He peers through the window of a boxy room along the corridor from where I met Ólafur. 'We will have a football hall there,' he says, pointing to a bobbly grass pitch. 'We signed the contract for it yesterday.'

Elegant furniture and oil paintings lend the room the appearance of a London club occupied by venerable gentlemen who clear their throats and crisply turn the pages of a broadsheet. It all came from Þorgrímur's house. He wanted to create a space at the club to relax and reflect, and to entertain visitors. And, as an acclaimed author of children's fiction, it is little surprise that a bookcase covers one wall.

Þorgrímur has been involved with the national team since 2007. He initially formed part of the delegation of luminaries who travel with the team for stuffy lunches and schmoozing. Lars Lagerbäck made him part of the backroom staff at the request of the players.

His exact role is hard to define, not least because he prefers to leave it vague. 'I always say when people ask me about my role, that I want to be the guy behind the scenes. I don't want to be in interviews.'

I was introduced to Þorgrímur by Ólafur Stefánsson, the philosophical captain of the Iceland handball team that won the Olympic silver medal. Ólafur compared his friend to a benevolent Keyser Söze – the elusive villain in *The Usual Suspects* – who orchestrates events from behind the stage curtain. Þorgrímur relishes the opaqueness. After we met I sent him a message to thank him for his time. 'Thanks,' he responded. 'I want to be modest and not too visible.' So what does he do?

'I'm the guy at the national team who tries to talk about mental value,' he says. 'Be a great person every day. Do ten things during the day to keep your peak state of mind. Don't be at your peak state of mind when you're at training, then go home and drink alcohol, smoke and hit your wife. Be perfect athletes in everything you do.'

He sits with his back to the window. The sunlight casts his face into shadow. His air is statesmanlike, with one leg primly crossed over the other. Indeed, he announced his intention to run for the Icelandic presidency in 2016 but pulled out when he realised how much it would intrude on his role with the national team.

Although he helps to carry the cones, Þorgrímur is not a coach. That makes it easier for players to talk to him, to use him as a sounding board. He does not have a hand in team selection but, as a former international, he is one of them. He appreciates the need for discretion in professional sport. He knows who will silently stew after a defeat and who needs whispered encouragement. Distance from nuts-and-bolts coaching gives him freedom to improve players in less tangible ways.

'I can't help them be better footballers, so I try to make them better people. If you make progress in eating, meditation, sleeping, reading books, being kind, all of a sudden you're 20 per cent better as a person. And if you're 20 per cent better as a person you become 20 per cent better as a footballer because you have better balance. It goes to your mind. I work on these things with the players. I'm not a psychiatrist. I'm nothing like that. I just believe that doing good deeds and being a good person helps with your career.'

Þorgrímur always provides quotations for the players to absorb. 'I put up lots of different quotes from great people, great thinkers. When the players go for a massage, they read [one of these quotes] and it goes up here.' He taps his forefinger against his temple. 'They may not know that they're reading it, but they read it anyway and the subconscious grabs something.'

He travelled to Russia with the chef and the kit manager several days before the team arrived for the

World Cup. That was when he pinned the quotations to the wall. Þorgrímur had a different selection – picked from the bookcase behind me – for every match. He does this because he believes players need to be able to imagine the taste of success.

'If you want to experience something in life you have to see it in front of you. Perhaps take a picture and put it on the wall. Look at it every now and then, and the dream goes here.' He pumps his fist against his heart. 'You have to visualise to get results later on.'

The players poke gentle fun at Þorgrímur. Gylfi jokes that if anyone struggles to sleep, they should read a few pages of one of Þorgrímur's books. Although his position as a quasi-life coach may seem glib, the players value his presence and the consistency it brings. While some may not readily admit it in a sport that still views intellectualism with suspicion, they embrace the literature he recommends. He arrived in France for Euro 2016 with 20 copies of *The Monk Who Sold His Ferrari* by Robin Sharma, in which the protagonist sells his supercar and embarks on a spiritual journey to the Himalayas. All the copies were claimed by the end of the tournament.

Þorgrímur admires the steely attitude he sees in the players, regardless of whether he has enhanced it.

'I will always remember the time we played against England,' he says. 'We had six days to prepare and at no point did I see fear in the eyes of the players. Never. They were just excited. "How many days left? When are we going to beat them?" That was the attitude. So the players run on to the pitch as winners, not questioning what the score will be.

'I think it started against Switzerland, the 4-4 match,' he muses, referring to when Iceland salvaged a draw in Basel despite trailing 4-1 in the second half. 'That was the moment the self-confidence went *crack!* "Yes, you guys, we can do it. Home or away. It doesn't matter."'

In a team sport increasingly influenced by individual accolades, Þorgrímur contends that friendship is at the centre of Iceland's success.

'Most journalists who come to make documentaries about Iceland go to the football halls. They think the indoor pitches made the players. That's wrong. The chemistry is the reason for the team doing so well.'

Ben Darwin agrees with Þorgrímur's identification of 'chemistry' in the Icelandic recipe, but the two men interpret the same word in different ways. For the urbane Icelander it is the essence of the vibe in the squad; for Ben, chemistry is quantifiable, and Iceland are successful because they are 'cohesive'.

'We'll speak to people who put success down to the water in the river, Icelandic spirit, or genetic disposition,' he says in an Australian drawl. 'We'll say: "I'm sorry, but that's bullshit. There's just no evidence that that's the case."'

Ben is a former professional rugby player who won 28 caps for Australia. The last of those came against New Zealand in the semi-final of the 2003 World Cup. A scrum collapsed and Ben's neck bore the weight. He suffered a serious spinal injury but avoided paralysis. At 26, though, his playing career was over. Early retirement presented Ben with the chance to reflect on the trajectory of his career. He played for the Brumbies at club level and

Australia internationally. Both sides outperformed their resources. Why?

'For every one player like me in Australia, there were ten or 15 of me in England,' Ben explains on a Skype call that crosses the hemispheres. 'I was confused as to why they weren't better as a collective. If it was such a competitive environment, why weren't they better?'

That question stewed in his mind during an eight-year coaching career at clubs in Australia and Japan. Some of those clubs had meagre resources but won everything, while others recruited lavishly only for their enviable squads to underperform. The impact of coaching and budgets seemed negligible. Abrupt unemployment gave Ben the opportunity to explore the variance in results.

'In 2013 I was fired from my job in Japan. The easiest thing to do when you get fired from a job is to go and start a consultancy company.'

A consultancy called Gain Line Analytics was the result. It emerged from a belief that there is a fundamental misunderstanding about why teams – in any sport – win matches. Ben suggests that a football team is made up of a network of relationships between players. The strength of those relationships – the cohesion – determines how a team will perform.

The performance analyst Simon Strachan joined Ben at Gain Line. Simon is also on our Skype call. Pat Ferguson, a doctoral candidate at Harvard with a background in econometrics, completed the team. After studying over 30 years of data from nine sports, the trio created the Team Work Index (TWI), a patented algorithm that calculates the quality and strength of the relationships in a team by looking at the experiences players have shared. In short, the TWI quantifies cohesion, and finds that it impacts on performance by up to 40 per cent.

The benefits of high cohesion are significant in international football because teams spend little time together and, consequently, average cohesion is low. Patience and continuity are both fundamental. To be brave is often to do nothing. But that goes against the grain in football, which has a culture of churn.

Different relationships carry different weight. A goalkeeper, for example, does not associate much with a striker, whereas a centre-half partnership requires intuitive understanding and constant communication. Iceland have strong relationships in the areas that matter. Gylfi and Aron have played in tandem since they were 17. The two centre-backs – Ragnar Sigurðsson and Sverrir Ingi Ingason – played together at club level for FC Rostov in the Russian Premier League in the months leading up to the 2018 World Cup. Though it is one of many elements in the algorithm, that week-in-week-out consistency benefits Iceland. The players sometimes pass the time by imagining what it would be like to buy a club and play together every week. If the Iceland squad were to follow through on that chit-chat, their cohesion levels would surge.

Even so, when Iceland beat England on the French Riviera in 2016 – with the five players from the same under-21 group in the line-up – Ben calculated a 260 per cent difference in cohesion between the two sides. No prizes for guessing which team scored high. The English players, Ben joked, looked like they had taken out restraining orders on each other when compared to Iceland, even though five of the team came from Tottenham Hotspur.

The young goalkeeper Rúnar Alex Rúnarsson noticed the cohesion in the Iceland team when he made his debut in 2017.

'It's a team that's built on relationships,' he affirms. 'It's pretty much the same 11 or 12 players that play all the time. They know exactly what everyone on the team is going to do. If you come in as a new guy, you have to adapt really quickly.'

The coach matters, too. Sir Alex Ferguson's departure from Manchester United is instructive: Ferguson left a high-cohesion team to David Moyes, who promptly made sweeping changes; performances then dropped while the players adapted and Moyes lost his job. Ben is only half joking when he says Moyes would have been more successful if he sat in the stands eating chips and left the players to it.

The Iceland team has changed little in terms of personnel or tactics since 2012. Many of the players had shared experience going back to their teenage years. Ólafur Jóhannesson may doubt his own contribution. His decision to promote talented youngsters en masse from the under-21s may have been the last, desperate roll of the dice. But it made Iceland cohesive.

'Cohesion doesn't mean Iceland will beat England,' Ben clarifies, 'it just gives them a chance.'

He uses a simple formula: skill x cohesion = capacity.

'Cohesion gives a team the capacity to be able to perform,' Simon adds. 'Without cohesion you've got no chance. With cohesion you've got the capacity.'

Iceland's cohesion allows them to bridge the talent gap with bigger nations. Moreover, what appears to be a disadvantage for Iceland actually works in their favour.

'If you look at it from an Icelandic perspective,' Ben says, 'the issue around coaching is limitations. What we find a lot of the time is that people in small systems simply don't have a choice. This is what happened with Iceland. There was no one left to pick. What happens when there's no one left to pick? You keep picking the same people. What happens when you keep picking the same people? They get better, they work harder for each other, and they start to mould on to each other from a performance perspective. Sometimes the miracle is the lack of choice. What we found is that there is a competitive advantage in lack of size and lack of resources.'

Simon adds: 'Nobody in Iceland would have said, "Let's pick from 30 blokes because this will give us the best advantage." The situation has created the perfect model for them.'

A life spent in elite sport has taught Ben that high performers are often normal people in interesting situations. He is not comfortable with the term 'golden generation'. 'It attaches something to those individuals that can't be repeated,' he reasons. 'It's as if there is something magical about them. Statistically I think there's something different about them and that is hard to replicate. But it's certainly plausible to rebuild again.'

Iceland players repeat how close-knit the squad is and this is reflected in their communication on the pitch. The sociologist Viðar Halldórsson analysed symbolic communication between players during the World Cup match between Iceland and Argentina. He found that Icelandic players made 81 positive gestures – ranging from high-fives to pats on the back – compared to 25 by their Argentine opponents. The Icelanders celebrated their small victories, the blocks and the defensive headers, while the Argentines grew frustrated at their failed attempts to break down the underdog.

Birkir Már Sæversson – a senior member of the group – says going on international duty is like meeting up with 22 brothers. But does friendship increase cohesion?

'Liking each other and being good mates can't be bad,' Simon responds. 'But there are plenty of examples of teams that hate each other's guts off the field yet are still very functional on the field.'

Ben elaborates: 'You can find lots of teams that are behaviourally destructive – from drug usage to illegal behaviour to terrible womanising – but incredibly successful and effective. The Mafia is a cohesive organisation. Bank robbers are cohesive.'

Friendship is a natural outcome of shared experiences on the pitch that demand players develop trust. Ben is reluctant, however, to attribute success to 'culture'. 'People use culture as a way of explaining something they can't measure or understand. What tends to happen is that high-cohesion teams have good culture because they've been together for so long that they form normative behaviours. Then people see those normative behaviours as the causation.'

Cohesion is objective. It can be measured. Culture cannot. 'It might piss people off,' Ben says, 'but it doesn't mean that I'm wrong.'

Some people use the 1988–90 generation as a crude explanation for Iceland's success. They point to the serendipity of such good players being born within two years of each other. While there is something in this explanation in terms of cohesion, we must treat it with care and acknowledge its limitations. It does not explain *why* these players emerged at the same time. The answer to that lies in a combination of better coaches, better facilities, a gritty mentality and networks. These players are the *result* of the good health of Icelandic football, rather than the cause. Once they emerged as talented teenagers, circumstance fell in their favour. Ólafur Jóhannesson gave them a chance. Lars Lagerbäck applied structure. Þorgrímur Þráinsson was the adhesive behind the scenes. They became cohesive.

## Chapter Eleven
# Euro 2016, narrated by Birkir Már Sævarsson

6 SEPTEMBER 2015. The final whistle went at Laugardalsvöllur to end a 0-0 draw with Kazakhstan. It was the most important moment in the history of Icelandic football. We were going to Euro 2016, our first major tournament. Do I remember it? Not really.

This was the first of a few blackout moments I would have in an Iceland shirt over the next year. I think I ran to Hannes Halldórsson, or maybe Kári Árnason, whoever was closest. We just hugged it out. It was unreal, partly because we had made history and partly because we were celebrating a 0-0 draw at home against Kazakhstan! It was such a bad game from us. We were so passive.

We still had two matches to play – away in Turkey and at home to Latvia – but in my head the Kazakhstan match was the last one. Those nine months between qualification and the tournament were a mix of excitement and anxiousness that I might pick up an injury. I was playing for Hammarby in Sweden, where the season starts in March and runs through the summer. I wasn't at my best in April and May. I didn't play badly, but nor did I play to my potential. It wasn't something I planned or wanted to do. It was like there was a brake on in the back of my head. My body didn't want to get injured.

I had made the right-back spot my own since Lars Lagerbäck took over, and I was confident that I would have a place in the squad for France. It's a cliché but you are never 100 per cent sure and you don't want to take anything for granted.

Two years later, when the squad for the 2018 World Cup was announced, I was eating lunch at the salt-distribution company I was working at. I had moved back to Valur by then. They are semi-professional and training doesn't start until five o'clock. I was going crazy at home and needed something to fill the day, so I got a job at my friend's company.

I'm not sure where I was for the squad announcement before the Euros, but I know that it was a bittersweet moment. I was relieved to be included, but my uncle, Gunnleifur Gunnleifsson, was left out. It came as a shock. He was devastated and I was devastated for him. He had been in the national team for such a long time and the Euros would have been the perfect ending. And he's family. Close family. I would have loved him to be there. We did get to play a few games together for the national team, soon after I made my debut in 2007. It was fantastic.

Just a few years before my Iceland debut, I had stopped thinking about becoming a professional footballer. I had stopped thinking about representing Iceland. I was working in a kindergarten, studying, and focusing on staying in the Valur team. Valur was my life when I was a kid. If I wasn't at school, I would be down at the club. I played football, handball, anything. We used to hide from the caretaker so he wouldn't kick us off the pitch.

But I had developed other interests by the time I was 16. I went a whole summer without playing football. I wanted to be a pilot. We all went on work placements when we were at school, at the age of 15. While the other kids went to some fancy bank, I went down to the airfield behind Valur's stadium to learn about air traffic control. I even did 45 hours of practical flying in a Cessna, but lacked the discipline to do the theory exams and get my pilot licence. I went back to football, but I have unfinished business with flying. I'm going to do an air traffic control course and that's what I plan to do after football.

Anyway, the Euros came around. No injuries, thankfully. I made an impact, and an unusual one for me, in one of the warm-up matches in Reykjavík. Lichtenstein were the opposition. We were winning 2-0. They cleared a corner and it bounced towards me. I hit it perfectly from 30 yards out, straight into the top corner. It was my first goal for Iceland. Heimir just stood on the touchline and laughed. Aron Gunnarsson was poking my head in the celebrations as if to say, 'YOU?' Nobody could believe I had done that. My shots usually go into Row Z.

We lost against Norway in the other friendly, which I think was actually a good thing. It gave us a kick up the butt. You can relax too much if you're easing through the friendlies, and that loss made us think, 'Woah, we need to step up here.'

The message from Lars and Heimir was consistent leading up to the tournament: 'Get through the group and everything else is a bonus.' We knew that if we could reach the knockout stage, we would be three matches from the final. Anything can happen in these tournaments. It comes down to your form on the day and how you wake up.

From the moment Lars arrived, he pounded into us that we could go far. He repeated it in hundreds of team meetings. It's a kind of brainwashing, but it worked. And the achievements of Greece in 2004 and Denmark in 1992 were in the back of our minds. There's always a small team that goes far. We believed it could be us.

I didn't feel nerves. There's always a butterfly in the stomach but I was just looking forward to it. We were making history, so what's the point in being nervous? You have to remember that it's football. It's the thing we love, and we were going to do it against the best teams in Europe, in a tournament, for the first time in Iceland's history. That's something to enjoy, not get nervous about.

First up: Portugal. What a match. I knew that I would be up against Cristiano Ronaldo. I don't usually focus too much on my opponent before a match, but I'd probably watched Ronaldo play about 300 times. My WhatsApp profile photo is of Ronaldo grasping at my shorts as I ran past him in a qualification match before Euro 2012. I might find a space on the wall for it when I quit football.

I knew him pretty well and I knew that I could keep him under control. That might sound a little cocky coming from someone who plays in Iceland, but I never doubt myself before a game. Honestly. I go into it thinking, 'I'm not going to make any mistakes and my player isn't going to score. If we concede, it won't be on me.' That's my mindset and I'm always confident that I'll see it through.

And I know that I can keep up with most. I once broke a treadmill in a little gym in Bolungarvík, the town on the Westfjords peninsula that my wife is from. I was running to keep in shape for pre-season and, all of a sudden, it stopped and didn't start again. It was probably old or something but I'll tell the fitness coach it was because of me.

Occasionally I visualise different scenarios in my head. Before away matches we have three or four hours to kill in the afternoon. I lie on my bed and try to relax. I see myself taking out Ronaldo or whoever I'm playing. I run through my plan to deal with my opponent.

With Ronaldo, you have to look for the weakest of his strengths. He's very good at cutting in on his right foot and shooting, so I tried to show him outside and force him to cross. Obviously he's a good crosser, but we've got two centre-halves inside the box who will head anything away. It helps that my team-mates, particularly Joey Guðmundsson and Aron, work so hard to support me. Being a defender in this team is pretty good. It's rare that I'm left one v one against a good winger.

The first wave of emotion came in the warm-up. There were 10,000 Icelanders singing 'Ég er kominn heim', a song about a guy coming home after a long time away. The message is that home is always there, waiting for you when you finish doing whatever you're doing. The rain was coming down. It made the hairs on the back of my neck stand up. My three eldest children, my wife and my mother were all in the crowd somewhere. I tried to pick them out before the match but it was impossible. Then came the national anthem. I usually keep my focus. I don't let the occasion affect me. This was different. People joke that my soul is black, but this time, it got me. An overwhelming feeling of pride.

Nani scored for Portugal after half an hour. Five minutes after half-time, Birkir equalised with a volley. It wasn't great defending from the Portuguese, not that we cared. The match finished 1-1. It was crucial to get that first goal of the tournament and finish the match feeling positive. If we had lost heavily ... well, you just don't know. It could have been devastating.

We heard about Ronaldo's comments when we were back in the dressing room. He criticised our 'small mentality' and defensive football. He said we'd go nowhere in the tournament. We laughed it off. For us, it was a case of 'job done' when we heard that. We knew that if he was complaining about our approach, it was because he was unhappy with the result and his own performance. We drove back to our training base at Annecy with any doubts gone. We felt like we could achieve something in France.

Returning to Annecy after each match was like returning to a home away from home. The hotel was perfect. The staff were lovely. Annecy itself is a little holiday town next to a lake. We would wander into town for a coffee and nobody would bother us. The place had a big impact on me. I'd love to go back there with my family for a proper holiday one day.

Cabin fever never became a problem. Not for me, at least. I shared a room with Ömmi Kristinsson, the back-up goalkeeper and my team-mate at Hammarby. We had some serious duels on the NHL PlayStation game. Þorgrímur Þráinsson, the man who does everything behind the scenes, organised a competition for us every day, all sorts of things from mini-golf to throwing socks into a bin. Everyone had to take part and he added up the scores at the end of the tournament and gave the winner a prize.

I can understand why some footballers find tournaments difficult. You're with the same people for several weeks in a high-pressure environment. It wasn't a problem for me. I'm a tolerant person. I'll put up with almost anything. Besides, when I meet up with these guys, it's like meeting up with 22 brothers. I'm so comfortable around them. They feel like family. That's what's so special about this group. I don't think many other national teams have the same spirit. We may have star players but they don't act like stars. They're as laid-back as the rest of us. It would have been normal to have at least one fight in training, or some kind of incident. But there was nothing. That's remarkable, really.

Next up: Hungary. This was the match that people back in Iceland expected us to win. It was described as the must-win match if we wanted to get out of the group.

It turned out to be our worst performance. Hungary had a lot of possession. We don't normally give a shit about possession statistics, but in this match we didn't come up and press. We weren't aggressive enough. Hungary outplayed us and created far too many chances. Despite all that, Gylfi put us ahead from the penalty spot and we still had that lead in the 88th minute.

And then ... the catastrophic moment for me. A low ball came through the six-yard box. I tucked in alongside Kári, a defensive movement that was second nature after so many years beside each other. I knew there was a Hungary player lurking behind me, ready to tap in at the far post. I had to stretch for the cross. It was a split-second decision. I threw myself towards the ball to send it back in the direction it had come from. But I couldn't reach. It deflected off the end of my toe. Pfft. It's hard to describe the feeling as the ball rolled over the line. I lay back and rested my head on the grass.

A few players gave me encouraging taps on the head. I watched the own goal after the match and realised that I couldn't have done much more. I had to go for it. If I had been lucky, the ball might have bounced up for Hannes. I didn't get lucky. Shit happens.

I try not to dwell on these things. I try not to overanalyse. We always have USB sticks available to us that contain our individual video clips from a match. I hardly ever watch them and it was no different after this game. The important thing was to concentrate on playing well against Austria.

The Austrians were our final opponents in the group stage. I sat in my usual seat on the bus on the way to the Stade de France. On the right, behind the middle door. Everyone has their seat. The cool kids sit at the back, the quieter ones towards the front. Even if we're driving the two-minute journey from the Hilton in Reykjavík to the national stadium, we all sit in our seats.

The other players went out on to the pitch to have a look around before we got changed for the warm-up. I stayed inside and drank a coffee, like I always do. I like the three minutes of solitude before everything starts to happen. I don't think of myself as a superstitious type. I don't put my right boot on before my left boot or anything like that, but I have my habits.

Aron Gunnarsson is the loudest voice in the dressing room, closely followed by Kári and Hannes. It's their way of motivating themselves. I'm the quiet guy. I never stand up and scream. It's not my style. I don't need to shout to motivate myself and nor do I need to be shouted at. I would feel uncomfortable with myself if I suddenly stood up and started screaming at people. I try to approach matches in a laid-back kind of way. It's football, not the end of the world.

We took the lead from a long throw-in. Kári glanced the ball at the near post and Jón Daði was waiting behind him to put it in the net. Practice makes perfect. We work on throw-ins in training. We have signals for the different routines. They're part of the set-piece sessions along with corners and free kicks. We thought that in this tournament other teams might be able to deal with it, but they couldn't. They all knew exactly what we were going to do and they still couldn't stop it.

Austria had a few chances to get back into it, and they won a penalty when Ari Freyr Skúlason held back David Alaba. It was a bit soft but Ari gave the referee the opportunity to give it. Aleksandar Dragović hit the post but the Austrians eventually equalised after an hour. A draw was enough for us to go through to the last 16. We were under a lot of pressure towards the end. Kári was blocking everything.

With the score at 1-1 in injury time, we went forwards on a counter-attack. Three of our players against one of theirs. I remember seeing the ball go across goal and past Birkir, to Arnór at the far post. The goalkeeper got a touch to his shot but it crept into the net. It was crazy. We all ran straight to the corner and the referee blew the final whistle there and then. We were celebrating wildly when we heard it go. Full time at the end of the England match was the purest moment of joy in the tournament, but this wasn't far behind.

When we were back on the bus, we heard about Gummi Ben's commentary of the winning goal: 'The voice has gone! But that doesn't matter! We have qualified! Arnór Ingvi Traustason scores! Iceland two, Austria one! What? The final whistle has been blown here, and never, ever have I felt so good!' I know Gummi well; most of us do. We played together at Valur. He called the moment perfectly.

England were up next. Playing them in a tournament was a massive deal. The English league is the one Icelanders watch above all others. We all support a team. We all have an opinion. I'm a Leeds United supporter. It's been a rough few years. Most of my family are Liverpool – my grandfathers, my mum, my wife. I have my dad to blame for following Leeds. He chose them in the early 1970s. English matches were available on Icelandic TV back then, but only one week after they were played. Leeds won the league in 1992, when I was eight. I thought they would be an easy team to support. My last trip to Elland Road was a 0-0 draw with Barnsley, so I got that wrong.

Again, there was no apprehension in the days leading up to the England match. Just excitement. Perhaps that was because of the clear message from Lars and Heimir: England were overrated. It wasn't about belittling or disrespecting England; we knew they had good players. But Lars and Heimir made us believe that we, as a unit, were just as good. England might have the star players and the individual skill, but we were the better team.

Lars added fuel to the fire when he told us in a team meeting that Roy Hodgson had not been at the Stade de France to watch our final group match, instead choosing to take his assistant on a cruise of the River Seine. We didn't quite go as far as to stick it to the dressing-room wall, but we certainly used it as motivation. The English thought they were going to cruise past us. We were determined to show them otherwise.

We made the worst possible start. After three minutes Raheem Sterling drifted inside off my wing. I should have kept an eye on him. I was ball-watching for a second too long and you can't do that at this level. All of a sudden he was in front of me. He took the ball around Hannes and won a penalty, which Rooney scored. Maybe, at that moment, England thought the game was over and that goals two and three would come by themselves. Maybe they relaxed too much.

Two minutes later, we were level. Our old friend came to the rescue: the long-throw routine. Aron threw it to Kári, who nodded it on for Ragnar Sigurðsson to score. It was important to get that equaliser quickly. It's in our nature, too. We've always been good at 'resetting' after we concede or score a goal. We reset and continue as if nothing had happened. A lot of small teams would have given up but it didn't matter to us. We always needed to score at some point if we were going to win the game.

We made it 2-1 soon after. Kolbeinn Sigþórsson scored after the ball slipped through Joe Hart's fingers. Part of me wanted Hart to parry the ball because I was waiting just to his left, ready to score the rebound!

We could see in the England players' eyes that they were stressed and frightened. 'What will the press say if we lose to Iceland?' That was probably what they were thinking. The first 80 minutes in Nice were the easiest of the tournament. Everything we did worked perfectly. Every single one of us played to our full potential. I felt like England were never going to score, and that's an amazing feeling. We limited them to long shots and created more chances of our own; even I had one with my mighty left foot.

Things changed when Marcus Rashford came on with ten minutes remaining. He was fresh and our legs were tired. Rashford kept picking the ball up in the space between Joey and me.

I couldn't go all the way up to meet him because I would have left space behind me, and if Joey had dropped deeper, the left-back would have been free. So every time Rashford got the ball, he was able to work up some pace. We barely managed to stop him. If I were the England coach, and it's easy to be wise with hindsight, I would have brought Rashford on earlier. He blew up the game. If he had been there from the 70th minute, he may well have created something.

But he didn't. The final whistle blew. It was another of those blackout moments. We were in our own half when the referee ended the game and the Iceland fans were at the other end. I sprinted straight over and started celebrating. The English didn't even cross my mind. One player came over to shake our hands and thank us for the game. I think it was Danny Rose. The rest of them just lay on the grass. The England shirt seemed pretty heavy.

I wanted to share the moment with my family. I grabbed my son and carried him over the barrier so he could see things from the other side. I had to put him back in the stands pretty quickly, there were so many cameras and people and he got a little shy.

After the initial blackout joy had faded it was time for the 'Viking clap'. There's nothing like it. It brings the players and the fans together in a unique way. There were some pretty good ones throughout the tournament but this one was special. It was a huge moment.

We allowed ourselves a few beers back at the hotel. You have to enjoy yourself, after all. You can't take it all too seriously. And with Snapchat and everything, we knew that it was absolutely crazy back at home. I don't know what day of the week it was, whether it was the weekend or a workday, but it seemed like everyone was out partying anyway.

The hosts, France, awaited in the quarter-final. The first half was a complete disaster. We were losing 4-0 after 45 minutes. France allowed us to bring the ball out a little and then they punished us on the counter. We conceded twice from set pieces. That's not like us. Other goals were preventable, too. Two of our players challenged for the same ball in the build-up to France's third goal, which Dimitri Payet scored. And they kept getting in behind us. That never usually happens. We never give away one-on-one chances.

Kolbeinn and Birkir Bjarnason scored for us but France were always out of reach. They had a clear tactical plan and executed it perfectly. If you judge them player by player they're probably not much better than England, but they were better prepared.

What a shit game. That was our initial reaction. We were frustrated. We conceded soft goals and that isn't in our nature. Perhaps, in the back of our heads, we were already happy with what we had achieved in France, and our motivation levels slipped.

We had maintained the same intensity in training. We kept working. Without getting too nationalistic, the Viking sleeve tattoo on my arm reminds me that we want to be tough, we want to be hard workers. But maybe after all the emotion of the England match, we were mentally drained. Maybe we didn't motivate ourselves enough to go out and give a good performance against France.

There was an element of physical tiredness as well. The same players started every match. We didn't have a dedicated fitness coach at the time, nor did we have the technology to monitor our heart rates and distances covered in training. It was a case of the coaches and physios asking, 'How are you feeling?' Obviously, they didn't get honest answers. Players will always lie a little about their condition, especially in a tournament. Nobody is going to say they don't feel fit to play.

Ten minutes after the final whistle that frustration turned to pride. We stood in front of 10,000 Icelandic supporters in an amazing stadium, having just made it to the quarter-finals of the Euros. How could we not be proud?

We were able to look at the bigger picture when we got back to the dressing room. Clearly, we weren't happy with the first half. But I don't think anybody was talking about the match. It was all about the tournament in general and the impact we'd made.

It was emotional for reasons beyond the results. We didn't know at the time that Lars would leave after the tournament. But we knew it would be Eiður Guðjohnsen's final trip with the national team. He had already quit once before, after we lost to Croatia in the play-off for the 2014 World Cup. Now, his space on the back row of the bus would be vacant again. Most of the guys were just kids when he played for Chelsea and Barcelona. He was a childhood idol for them. Eiður became a link between the coaches and the players in France, but at the same time, he was always another one of the guys.

We knew there would be a reception for us back in Iceland. We didn't realise it would be as big as it was. It's about 50km from Keflavík airport to downtown Reykjavík. For most of that stretch of road there were cars and people on both sides, welcoming us home. It seemed like the entire country was waiting for us in Reykjavík. You couldn't see the ground through a sea of people in blue shirts. Everywhere you looked there were people. Maybe that's when it all sank in. I will never forget that. I will never forget the Euros. A happy memory that lasted for a month.

# Chapter Twelve

# Our girls

BEFORE ICELANDIC men won football matches, Icelandic women won football matches. The women's national team became the first from Iceland to qualify for a major tournament when they secured a place at the 2009 European Championship in Finland. Their male counterparts would not repeat the feat for another seven years.

Iceland won eight of ten qualifiers ahead of the tournament, yet still finished as runners-up to a formidable France side. A two-legged play-off against the Republic of Ireland beckoned. Iceland had been in the same position four years earlier. Euro 2005 was tantalisingly close until a disastrous 2-7 defeat to Norway in Reykjavík shattered the dream before the second leg. There were no such issues against Ireland. A 1-1 draw in Dublin set the stage for a finale in Reykjavík, where the Icelanders cruised to a 3-0 victory that made history. Margrét Lára Viðarsdóttir, Iceland's all-time leading goalscorer, finished that campaign with 12 goals, more than any other player in the entire qualification process.

*Stelpurnar okkar* ('our girls') were eliminated at the group stage in Finland after narrow defeats to Germany and Norway but carried their momentum through to qualification for the following competition, held in Sweden in 2013. Defeat to group winners Norway in the final round of fixtures forced Iceland back into the play-offs, where they dispatched Ukraine 6-4 on aggregate.

In Sweden they progressed from a fiendish group that pitted them against Germany and Norway, the eventual finalists. A 4-0 defeat to the hosts in the quarter-final was no disgrace, and Iceland qualified for a third consecutive tournament in 2017. It was the first time they had qualified automatically without having to win a play-off, but performances on the big stage were meek, and Iceland exited after finishing below Austria, France and Switzerland. Yet the sight of Iceland in the draw for a major tournament no longer causes a raised eyebrow. Indeed, throughout the last decade, the women's national team has consistently sat inside the top 20 in the FIFA rankings, reflecting their status among the established elite. For context, Iceland rank above Argentina, Portugal and Belgium.

Iceland have not yet made their debut at a World Cup, as so many UEFA nations compete for so few spots. But they have come close at the last three times of asking. As in qualifying for Euro 2009, Iceland won eight of ten matches ahead of the 2011 World Cup, only to finish behind France with just one team going through to the play-offs. It was a similar story four years later when Iceland finished as runners-up to Switzerland. Yet the cruellest result was still to come. They finished behind Germany in qualification for the 2019 World Cup and would have gone through to the play-offs as one of the best second-placed teams, were it not for a quirky rule that stipulated results against the bottom team in each group – the Faroe Islands in Iceland's case – did not count in the calculation.

This has all taken place in the context of a thriving domestic league, in which ten teams compete for a place in the Women's Champions League. Though there are a handful of foreign players from Azerbaijan to Mexico, the domestic league provides a strong platform for local players. At Euro 2017, 15 of the Iceland squad played for Icelandic clubs, with most of the other players scattered across the Scandinavian leagues.

Guðbjörg Gunnarsdóttir – goalkeeper for Iceland and Djurgårdens IF in Sweden – believes the success of the women's national team is a product of a progressive society.

'We had the first female president in the world and we had the first gay prime minister, who was also a woman. It's an Icelandic thing. In other parts of society women have been given bigger roles for a long time.'

She sits beside the satisfying order of a tactics whiteboard in a tranquil hotel in La Manga, where a Tetris landscape of whitewashed apartments interrupts the view of the Mediterranean blue. It is late January and the Iceland women's squad have escaped to the temperate Spanish winter. Outside, in the marble-clad corridor, faceless mannequins model polo shirts to visiting golfers.

'It's not like the guys are kings and we're not,' Guðbjörg says. 'We feel very respected and that comes from the whole society.'

It is an easy case to make. Iceland is, demonstrably, the best place in the world to be a woman. The World Economic Forum's Global Gender Gap report measures the differences between men and women in politics, education, health and economics in 144 countries. Iceland had the best overall score in 2017 – for the ninth consecutive year.

An autumnal Friday in 1975 was a defining moment for the emancipation of Icelandic women. On 24 October an estimated 90 per cent of women took the day off. Having grown weary of unequal wages, women did not go to work or do housework. Twenty-five thousand people gathered in Reykjavík to deliver speeches. That was almost a quarter of the city's population. It is also remembered as the day Iceland ran out of sausages, as there were no workers to process the meat in the factory. The babble and shriek of playing children wafted into households because male radio presenters were forced to look after their children in the studio.

A theatre manager called Vigdís Finnbogadóttir was among the throng. Five years later she became the first democratically elected female president in the world. Incidentally, one of her rivals in the 1980 election was Albert Guðmundsson, the first professional footballer from Iceland. Vigdís held office for 16 years and normalised the sight of women in positions of power. Speaking to the BBC in 2017, she recalled an anecdote about an Icelandic boy who saw Ronald Reagan as the president of the United States on television. 'Mummy! Mummy!' he exclaimed, 'Can a man be a president?'

The KSÍ is aware of its place within this tradition and has sought to remove institutionalised inequality in football. In early 2018, shortly before the Iceland women's squad convened at La Manga, the KSÍ announced that it would pay equal bonuses to the men's and women's teams. Guðbjörg and her team-mates appreciate the gesture. But, as an economics graduate, she understands that the disparity begins far higher than the KSÍ.

'Of course we get less money,' she says with rueful conviction. 'There's an astronomical difference in what UEFA pays if the guys get to the World Cup versus if we get to the World Cup. If we get to the same competition as the guys, the KSÍ gets 3 per cent of what it gets from the guys doing the same. So the KSÍ has to pay us from its own pocket.'

The Iceland captain Sara Björk Gunnarsdóttir played for Wolfsburg against Lyon in the final of the 2018 Women's Champions League. As in the men's game, it is the biggest prize in club football. According to the BBC, UEFA paid the winner of the 2017 women's version £219,920, while the winners of the men's version received £13.5 million.

'I think it's crazy that there's such a difference,' Guðbjörg says. 'I understand that it's about popularity, sponsorship and the media. But at the same time, women's football is something that can really sell. It's a product, as we saw at the 2017 Euros in Holland. When Holland won it was crazy. They were like superstars.'

Guðbjörg talks fluidly, pausing once to remember a word that has become instinctive in Swedish but rusty in English. She accepts that big, non-Icelandic clubs want to maximise the return on their investment at first-team level. She is wary of tokenism but laments a reluctance to invest in grassroots women's football.

'[Professional and grassroots football] are two very different things and we should think of them differently,' she says. 'We hear a lot of things like, "Why should we put money into the women's game when we don't get anything back?" as if it's just about the cost. I think that's so wrong and sad.'

What is the solution? 'I think you could delete the problem if you marketed the product better. Why should a father with one son and one daughter only go to a men's game at the weekend? Why wouldn't you want your daughter to see girls playing and have role models, as you want your son to have role models? I think the biggest thing is to get into the heads of the parents. It's so brutal if a daughter can't go with her parents to a women's game but the son can always go with his dad to watch a men's game. It's a habit.'

That habit is eroding in Iceland. In August 2018, over 9,000 supporters crammed into Laugardalsvöllur to watch the women's national team play Germany. That is like the England women's team playing to a sell-out crowd at Wembley Stadium.

'The KSÍ has much better marketing around the team and so many more people watch the games,' says Guðbjörg. 'When I started in 2004 there was almost nobody. There was one small advertisement that said, "There's a game on tomorrow." Nobody really cared. Now everyone is there. We feel the pressure and the KSÍ doesn't have to make the same effort to attract people. They come because they want to and this is all through marketing.'

Fewer empty seats are not the only thing that has changed. When Guðbjörg made her debut in 2004, the women's team was effectively only 12 years old. Though originally formed in 1981, the parlous finances of the KSÍ meant the team was disbanded six years later. They did not play again until 1992. Guðbjörg describes the transformation since she started as 'like black and white'. There are more training camps and more staff; a full squad travels to away matches, rather than the paltry 16 players that the budget once allowed. The dark-blue tracksuit Guðbjörg wears is a personal symbol of rapid professionalisation.

'A lot of things changed between the European Championships in 2009 and 2013. We were such amateurs in 2009. It was our first time at a tournament and we were just so happy to be there. We just thought, "Oh, we get all these clothes!" We didn't even understand that we could get money for being there.

'I think it changed across Europe. The marketing of Sweden 2013 was much better than Finland 2009. The game was getting much, much bigger. The difference between Sweden and Holland 2017 was the same again. The people following us in 2009 were boyfriends, family and close friends. It was 50 people or something. Then, in 2013, there were so many people coming. And in 2017 half the nation came! It felt like everyone who couldn't afford to watch the guys in France came to Holland to follow us.'

Women footballers have become as ubiquitous as the men in Iceland. They are just as likely to appear emblazoned on a billboard promoting Coca-Cola's cool commercialism. The women's national team even altered the course of colloquial language. The phrase *spila eins og kerlingar* ('to play like chicks') was common parlance to deride a poor performance by the men's team. After 2009 it became a light-hearted, if rather awful, expression of positivity. Playing like the chicks meant winning matches.

'Unstoppable For Iceland', the commercial released by Iceland Air to coincide with the 2017 European Championship, knits together the against-all-odds stories of three girls who are on the periphery of football; outsiders peering in. The first girl leans against a peeling goalpost while the boys play at full throttle. 'Next time you'll definitely be allowed to play,' her brother assures her on the windswept walk home. The second girl dusts off her hands after a tracksuit-clad thug administers a shove in the back and follows it up with a callous smirk that makes it clear she is not welcome. The third girl glances enviously as her brother unwraps a pair of Adidas football boots for Christmas. She had been given ballet shoes, glittery and girly. The soundtrack of mournful string instruments fades. 'Never Let Adversity Prevail' – a message with deep roots in the Icelandic psyche – appears on the screen as a rousing drumbeat reaches a crescendo. Footage of the three girls is spliced with the women's national team in a pre-match huddle.

The video depicts a reality that has faded into the mists of time – in Iceland, at least. Access to football is open, even if for Guðbjörg 'indoor' training could only begin once dressage jumps were removed from the gravelly equestrian hall that provided primitive shelter from the elements. Just like Icelandic boys, girls now train in modern facilities with qualified coaches.

A brief scene in 'Unstoppable For Iceland' shows two youth teams, each on a podium as they celebrate victory in a

tournament. One is a girls' team, one a boys' team. On first glance they are identical. A replay reveals that the boys hold aloft a big-ears trophy while the girls have a small vase. As Guðbjörg explains, there is an anecdote behind the scene.

'It's easy to fix problems because it's such a small country. If someone writes something on Facebook the media are on it. I remember reading an interesting Facebook status from a mother who had a son and a daughter who were both extremely good at football. The boy was the best player at a tournament and he won a really big cup. The next weekend the girl was the best player, but she got a really small prize.

'The mother wrote: "What is this? Who is deciding this?" Everyone went totally crazy and asked who had arranged the cups. There was also a TV programme filming the guys' tournament but not the girls'. It was enough for the mother to write that status. An angry housewife writes a status, the media sees it, and it's a big article. Then it's at the table of the education and sports minister.

'If something like this happens everyone gets so angry, so it's fixed. It can be an issue so much faster in a small country, and I think we're quite pushy here. In bigger countries all this takes time and nobody dares to say anything.'

The women's game keeps its feet firmly planted in the real world. Most of the players on the training camp in La Manga are semi-professional. We are sat in the team meeting room. On the other side of a wicker partition that is stretched like a concertina, half a dozen players hunch over textbooks. Some are studying for university exams. Others are still at school.

Guðbjörg views their graft through her present situation. Her 30th birthday – a jarring milestone for all footballers – delivered a reminder of the transitory nature of a professional career and prompted a job hunt that led to part-time work at an economic consultancy in Stockholm.

'Guys would never have to do anything else on the side,' she says, 'and I don't know if they would want to. Personally, I think that can be bad for the guys. They're empty when their careers are over because they haven't done anything else for such a long time. It makes the transition hard. You can see that more male players than female struggle with alcohol and drugs after their careers, because women are more used to having to work, or give birth. We have to fight a little bit more for our existence.'

Freyr Alexandersson – the head coach of the women's national team from 2013 to 2018 – has an olive complexion more native to La Manga than Iceland. He spent the majority of his career as a sturdy centre-half in the Icelandic Second Division. Now in his mid-thirties, he still carries himself with the coiled poise of someone who always wins the second ball.

He reclines with a thick black coffee while his players squirrel away at their studies on the other side of the concertina partition.

'Back home they're high profile,' he says, throwing a nonchalant thumb over his shoulder in their direction. 'Everybody knows them and we want it to be like that. Expectation makes us better. I wouldn't coach the women's team if there were no expectations and nobody cared.'

Freyr's words carry the conviction of ambition. In August 2018 he became the assistant coach to Erik Hamrén, the Swede who replaced Heimir Hallgrímsson as coach of the men's team. Freyr stepped down from the women's team the following month. It would come as little surprise if he were to succeed Hamrén, as Heimir succeeded Lars Lagerbäck in 2016.

His focus has oscillated between men's and women's football.

'A few years ago I thought I coached men and women in the same way,' he says. 'In recent years I've thought about it and I think I change myself a little bit. The approach is not that different but you need to be more specific about tactical principles in the women's game. Overall if you have 23 top-quality men and 23 top-quality women, most of the men will have a higher football IQ. That's a fact. I think it comes down to men watching football more, sometimes too much. So I go into a little bit more detail with the women's teams.

'How I approach them at the training ground is not that different. I coach at the highest level in the women's game so I just approach them as professional footballers. Sometimes the women's team have felt like I pushed them a little too much, but they got used to it and started to like it. Now they wouldn't have it any other way.'

Like most employees of the KSÍ, Freyr has juggled several jobs. While he coached the women's team he ran sessions for the men and worked as an opposition scout for the men's team in the months preceding the 2018 World Cup. He sees the men and women as two cuts of the same cloth.

'They're both strong-mentality groups with good humour and they're proud to be in the national team. They act in the same way as a group. It's the same banter, more or less. The only difference is that the guys would not be studying out there. They would be playing Nintendo Switch or something. That's the reality they live in.

'I think the guys really respect the women. They're so proud of them, and vice versa. The guys talk to me and they follow the women's team closely. They know every player and all the results.'

There are bonds between the two teams that extend beyond the kroner in their bonus package. They stay in the same hotel in Reykjavík when the fixture schedule permits. Hannes Halldórsson and Guðbjörg – the goalkeepers' union – trade tips on gloves and treatment for dislocated shoulders. It is hard to imagine Manuel Neuer or David de Gea exchanging advice with their counterparts in the women's team.

While Freyr refines players at the top of their game, equally impressive coaches work to extend the reach of girls' football.

In his former role as the head of youth development at the KSÍ, Þorlákur Árnason was responsible for girls' and boys' football. In April 2018, he opened a blog entry by explaining that he had led a talent-identification programme for girls and boys between the ages of 13 and 15.

'I discovered how big a difference there is between the two genders at this age,' he wrote. 'Girls reach puberty approximately two years ahead of boys. But are we really acknowledging that fact and using that information to train girls all over the world?'

In Iceland, the average girl experiences the most growth at 11.58 years of age, while the average boy will not have their spurt until 13.85 years old. Þorlákur repeatedly refers to the 'golden age', the period in which children learn fastest and are most receptive to coaching because beanpole growth has not yet unsettled their coordination. He contends that girls start playing football too late.

'Because their golden age is between eight and ten years old, girls need to start when they are five or six in order to develop certain skills before they enter the period in which their coordination and control of movement is at its best. Give this some thought: starting at seven or eight means girls will be beginners when they hit the period in which they can learn the most! Boys are rarely beginners when they reach this period because they start earlier and develop later. On average, boys have played football for five years when they hit their "golden age", while girls have one or two years of football experience when they hit theirs.

'So let's start the revolution,' he concludes. 'Get the girls on the football field earlier. Not because I am telling you, but because science is telling you.'

The parallel solution, as Þorlákur sees it, is to ensure girls aged between eight and ten have excellent coaches. The ubiquity of women's football eases the task in Iceland. It is not viewed as a poor relation to the men's game, and coaches – particularly perceptive coaches actively seek to improve girls during their footballing 'golden age' – tend to train both boys and girls.

The former head of youth at Breiðablik, Daði Rafnsson, coached Jiangsu Suning's women's team in China before returning to Iceland to work on a PhD in mental strength in sport. Before that, in 2009, he asked to coach the girls' under-ten team at Breiðablik.

'I thought it was a challenging project,' he says. 'There was a vast difference in ability between boys and girls at 16 years old. I thought, "Why?" There isn't much physical difference, so it must be cultural.

'I watched what the under-ten boys were doing – drills, keep-ups, difficult shooting practices. They were encouraged to use their left and right feet, they were doing two-v-one situations, wall passes, all this. The under-ten girls were doing nothing like that. They were basically doing games without the balls, without being encouraged to do difficult things.'

Daði introduced more challenging training and, predictably, the group's technical and tactical aptitude improved.

Looking forwards, the KSÍ must encourage more female coaches to attend UEFA courses. About one in ten Icelandic coaches are women. Although that ratio is better than almost every other country, it lags behind other areas of society in terms of representation.

Although Iceland is the best country in the world to be a woman, and probably one of the best to be a woman who aspires to be a professional footballer, it is not perfect. There is a temptation to romanticise a continuous thread of gender equality in Iceland that stems from the formidable women of the Sagas. That narrative overlooks, among other things, Icelandic governmental policy during and immediately after the Second World War. Women who socialised with occupying soldiers were exiled to rural areas, purportedly for their own good and the good of the nation.

The Icelandic government went as far as to request that the American forces did not station black troops at its airbase near Keflavík. As the historian Valur Ingimundarson writes: 'It was felt that the nation's interests would be best served if miscegenation, i.e. relations between black men and Icelandic women, could be avoided.' This archaic racist policy – offensive to the black men it demonised and to the Icelandic women it demeaned – lasted until the 1960s.

Iceland is not immune to the problems that blight the rest of the world. In January 2018, 462 female athletes signed a statement that condemned gender-based discrimination, harassment and sexual violence. The statement included 62 personal accounts of abuse. Football was not specifically implicated – no individual sport was named – yet it is difficult to conceive that none of the 462 women were footballers.

One sportswoman shared a particularly egregious account of being raped by her coach on the day of a match. 'It's a game day,' she wrote. 'It's Sunday morning and there's nobody else in the gym. I'm alone at a meeting with the coach before we're all supposed to meet for the game. He rapes me. Not the first time and not the last. I was then scolded by the coach for coming one minute late into the meeting.'

The statement landed on the desk of Lilja Alfreðsdóttir, the Minister of Education, Science and Culture; a position that also covers sport. Her response was swift.

'The women came forward and we had a meeting the day after, which I chaired. We immediately established a working group with all the key stakeholders. I am extremely grateful to the women who stepped forward because it was not easy. The disadvantage of being in such a small community is that everyone knows everyone. Some of the cases are just horrible.'

The passage of time will reveal whether Iceland eradicates this abuse. With campaigns like the #MeToo movement providing a platform for people to show solidarity, the pincers of condemnation are closing on men who abuse positions of power with impunity.

It would be remiss to close on such a negative note. When faced with one of the most equal, supportive societies in the world, our instinct is to feel for the imperfections. Iceland is not perfect but it is better than most. On 5 September 2018 two articles appeared on *The Guardian* website. The author of the first article was Hope Solo, the goalkeeper who played 202 times for the United States women's national team between 2000 and 2016. Her opening paragraph packs a punch:

'We called ourselves the Ponytail Posse because that's what the US women's national team was about. The white girls next door. You want statistics to back that up? Barely more than a dozen female players of colour have represented the United States at the highest level since 1991. Something is broken.'

The second story revealed that players from Crystal Palace Ladies were told they may not be able to represent the club if they failed to raise £250 each for subscription fees, either through sponsorship or out of their own pockets. It sent a negative message about the importance of the women's team to the club as a whole, which was made starker by the £130,000-per-week contract Palace had handed to Wilfried Zaha – the star of the men's team – earlier that week. To Zaha's great credit, he made a significant donation to support the female players.

Those two stories lend perspective. Women's football in Iceland is healthy from the top down. It will continue to flourish with the dedication and emotional intelligence of coaches like Freyr, Daði and Þorlákur and role models like Guðbjörg.

'We have to fight a little bit more for our existence,' Guðbjörg said in La Manga. Women's football still faces a battle, but Iceland is on the front line.

## Chapter Thirteen
# Iceland v Croatia

AT THE end of the road is a soot-black beach. The sand twitches in the wind like a swarm of locusts fighting for lift-off. The first people to inhabit Vestmannaeyjar were Irish slaves seeking refuge in the settlement period. I understand their choice when I turn away from the wind and feel grains of sand crackle against my back. The swirl of sand erases footsteps laid 30 seconds earlier. Before ferries and flights, you could escape to Vestmannaeyjar and leave no trace.

The islands rise and fall like a seismograph on the dull horizon. June is a good time to visit; purple wildflowers are in bloom. My accommodation on Heimaey – the archipelago's only inhabited island – is homely. Bookcases cover three sides of my bedroom, densely packed with English and Icelandic literature. It is on the ground floor of Björg and Erpur's house, three streets back from the harbour.

Björg is a smiley woman with firefly eyes and a voice coarsened by cigarettes. She shows me upstairs to the living room. At the top of the stairs I find a dozen British people cramped around an elongated dining-room table. I recognise some of them from the ferry. A man with a grey beard ladles thick vegetable stew into a bowl. He takes a hunk of bread from a wooden board and passes it to his right. The Brits seem to know each other but not very well. I gather from the burble of conversation that most of the group work for the Royal Society for the Protection of Birds. They have come to spend ten days on Elliðaey – one of the uninhabited islands – to research the indigenous puffin population.

Björg's husband, Erpur, occupies the head of the table. His work as a leading academic in the research of puffins led the family to Vestmannaeyjar a little over a decade ago. One by one, the Brits pause from their stew to introduce themselves. They talk about their experience in ringing birds. Ten people speak. Then it is my turn.

'Most of that has gone over my head,' I confess, 'because I'm here to write a book about Icelandic football.'

A Californian woman to my right whoops and claps. The others nod and murmur.

'So are any of you big soccer fans?' Erpur asks. They all look around. They all say nothing. Wrong crowd.

A disproportionate number of Iceland's finest footballers hail from Vestmannaeyjar. On the men's side: Ásgeir Sigurvinsson, Hermann Hreiðarsson and Tryggvi Guðmundsson, the record scorer in the Icelandic First Division. On the women's side: Margrét Lára Viðarsdóttir, the record scorer for the national team. The men's and women's teams from ÍBV – the main club on

Vestmannaeyjar – both won the Icelandic Cup in 2017. As did the men's handball team the same year.

I have come to Vestmannaeyjar because people have told me it is a distilled version of Iceland. The small pool of players creates an enforced cohesion that leads to success. It is the same paradox that exists around the Iceland national team. Iceland uses its smallness to gain an advantage over larger nations, and the islanders adopt a similar approach to compete with better-resourced clubs on the mainland. It seemed a natural setting to watch Iceland's final group match of the World Cup.

Ian Jeffs juggles two roles at ÍBV: head of youth development and coach of the women's team. Jeffs first set foot on Vestmannaeyjar when he arrived on loan from Crewe Alexandra in 2003. He went on to play under Heimir Hallgrímsson across two spells in 2007 and 2011, while Heimir also assessed him for his UEFA coaching licences. 'You'd never get that in England,' Jeffs says. 'Everyone knows everyone. Everyone has some connection.'

I ask him if people on Vestmannaeyjar see themselves as different to 'mainlanders'.

'Yeah, they do. It's built into their roots. It goes back to the past when travel from the island to the mainland was a lot more difficult than it is now. It wasn't just half an hour on the ferry, then an hour-and-a-half drive to Reykjavík. It used to be a boat, then a horse and cart.

'They say that footballers on this island need to be tough,' he adds. 'It took two days to play a football game, with travel. Even now, during the winter, you get coaches who come from Reykjavík and they're amazed at how difficult it is.

'Where they've got 100 kids in one age group, we've maybe got 20. And of that 20 we've got 18 who are practising both football and handball. Then again, something we have over them is more quality time with our kids. You're not going to leave Vestmannaeyjar to train with another club. That's impossible. That's our strength. We get to interact with the players more.'

Just as the coaches interact with the players, the town interacts with the club. ÍBV rely on sponsorship and financial support from the fishermen and other local companies. Those companies respond with remarkable generosity because it is their children who will benefit from ÍBV competing in the top division. It is their children who will benefit from the club hiring another youth coach.

Several years ago, a team from ÍBV was travelling back to the mainland ferry terminal after a victorious cup final. There was a party on the bus. Music blared. Seatbelts lay dormant. The jubilation disintegrated as a police siren howled over the music. A police officer came on board, but there were no arrests and no warnings; the officer came bearing a box of champagne and proceeded to offer an escort to the ferry. The officer was from Vestmannaeyjar and they look after their own.

One stormy evening in January of 1973, Påll drifted off to sleep early. It was 10pm, but darkness had fallen seven hours earlier. Home was the west side of Heimaey – the most westerly street in the town, in fact. Påll worked as the technical engineer on the island. His two young children slept in the next room. His wife was out visiting her cousin in the centre of town. Påll awoke when she returned at midnight. He padded down the stairs, and they sat and talked.

'Did you feel those earthquakes earlier?' she asked.

'Nay, nay. Nothing.'

They changed the subject. After all, it was normal to feel murmurs in this part of Iceland, perched on the fault line where the Eurasian and North American tectonic plates jostle for position. Instead, Pàll's wife told him about the conversation she'd had with her cousin about the series of eruptions in 1963 that formed Surtsey, a new island a few miles south of Heimaey. Surtsey became the second-biggest island in the archipelago after it rose from the ocean just a decade ago. An island younger than they were – now that is something, they said. They peeked through the curtains. The bad weather had kept all the fishing boats in the harbour, so if anything like Surtsey were to happen again, the 5,000 people who lived on Heimaey would be able to sail to the mainland.

They went upstairs at about 1am. As Pàll settled on the bed, he felt the delicate rumble of another earthquake. His first thought was to make sure he had a roll of film in his camera. He was due to fly to Denmark, via Reykjavík, the following morning. If an eruption like the one that formed Surtsey were to happen while he was in the air, he wanted to be able to capture it.

Glancing out of the bedroom window, he saw an orange glow warming the winter horizon. It looked like a farm to the east of the town was on fire. The reality was far worse. A gaping fissure had opened on the far side of the island, lava spraying into the air. Eldfell – 'fire-mountain' – had awoken with a start.

The evacuation began immediately. Police cars careered through the gridded streets, their sirens piercing the night. Islanders began to drive down to the harbour and board the fishing boats to the mainland. It was the luckiest storm they could remember. If the weather had been calm, the fishermen would have been at sea and their families stranded beneath the eruption. But the boats were at home, their rigging clinking in the wind. They crossed the swell to Þorlákshöfn, 40km away. One of the evacuees was five-year-old Heimir Hallgrímsson. He was used to the fishing boats – his father fixed the nets used to haul in the catch.

I meet Páll in his office above the town bank, 45 years after that night. He is in his seventies now, but still works as a civil engineer. His lined face is kindly and his body rugged, the result of a morning routine that begins with a swim in the municipal pool at 6am.

'There was no panic,' Páll says, thinking back to that night in 1973. He stutters as his English warms up. 'Some people drove their families down to the harbour, then drove back home to put the car in the garage because they knew there would be ash fall.'

One teenager had an exam the day after the eruption. He took his revision material with him to the mainland. He thought he might return to Heimaey in time to put pen to paper. An older islander dashed home to pick up his cigarettes before boarding a fishing boat, only to forget his wallet, which was next to the pack of smokes.

Páll did not leave at all. When his wife and two children boarded a fishing boat to sail to the mainland, he stayed on the island, with the stormy skies and the rolling lava. His role as technical engineer demanded that he was one of the several dozen people to remain on the island that first night.

The final boat bobbed out of the harbour at 6am, four hours after the eruption. Páll went for a closer look that morning.

'We drove to the south of the island and saw where the fissure had opened,' he says. 'It got bigger and bigger. It was two kilometres in length and perhaps three metres wide.

'In the beginning the lava was just building up. It just went up a little. The ash went higher.' Páll does not embellish his speech with rich description or hyperbole. He deals in detail, the detail that was relevant to him on that morning. I ask if he felt scared and expect a stiff-upper-lip response.

'Scared? OK, of course you have some feeling of being afraid ...' He trails off, eager to show me something else. We walk along the corridor, past the topographical maps that track the ominous spread of the lava by date. The floorboards creak.

'The mayor's office was here,' he explains, leading me into a wood-panelled meeting room that smells of the past. 'The first meeting was held here, in this room, at ten o'clock in the morning. The city council came together: the mayor, the fire chief, the police chief, the doctor at the hospital, and me – the technical engineer.'

A grainy photo on the table captures the scene in black and white. Páll points himself out. He is the one with a shock of dark hair and a patterned jumper knitted in the Icelandic style. After the meeting, he was stationed at the harbour. The town owned a boat that had stayed after the evacuation. Páll sailed to the far side of the island to monitor the lava as it flowed towards where the sea licked the shore.

He places both palms on the table and peers down his light-blue sleeves to the photo. He leans back and looks at me. A thought enters his mind.

'Have you ever stood close to a house while it's burning?' he asks.

'No,' I reply, wondering where this is going.

'You think it will stop. In the beginning we thought that after a few hours, a few days, a few weeks, it would stop. That was at the beginning. When you see a house burning you think that it will stop without burning everything inside.'

Påll walks to the window. I look out and see the dark heart of Eldfell. It was exposed when one side of the mountain collapsed and rode away on the flow of lava. The volcano is blotchy, crimson and black. It still looks angry.

'At first we watched the eruption from here,' Påll explains. 'Then we put metal plates on the window.' Those metal plates shielded many east-facing houses in the first few days. The volcano spat red-hot rocks across the town. They smashed through windows and ignited what was inside. Påll remembers the rocks for another reason. 'Some of them were so hot,' he says as a grin spreads across his face. 'I smoked cigarettes back then and I could take a stone from the street and light my cigarette with it.'

At first, the wind was kind, blowing ash away from the town. But it changed direction after three days. At that point Påll and the other members of the rescue team erected supportive columns inside houses to stop the ceilings collapsing under the weight of the ash. Once the windows were fortified and the ceilings supported, the rescue team began gathering the possessions of those who had left. Abandoned cars filled the first few ships bound for the mainland. Furniture went next. Every house in the town was stripped and the contents packed into containers. A young man called Arnór was responsible for rescuing the pets that people had left behind. Budgies and cats were sent away to be reunited with their owners. Meanwhile, the journalists and film crews needed shepherding as Vestmannaeyjar challenged the Vietnam War for international attention.

The final containers left in April. But the lava kept flowing relentlessly. The rescue team fashioned makeshift barriers from ash and rocks; the lava broke through. They used bulldozers to make tracks into the molten rock; by the following day, the tracks had moved closer to the harbour.

The harbour was their main concern. Vestmannaeyjar was the hub of fishing in southern Iceland because the natural harbour was deep enough to accommodate the biggest vessels while providing shelter from the wind. It was sheltered from the wind because the entrance was narrow. As the entrance was narrow, the creeping lava threatened to close it forever. The island would wilt without the custom the harbour brings. Even those who are not at sea live off the catch, in the fish factories or the dry docks. The population had mushroomed from 600 to 2,400 in the first two decades of the 20th century as motorised fishing thrived. If the languid tsunami of lava continued, that number would plummet back down. The eruption posed an existential crisis.

The rescuers experimented with spraying seawater on the lava to cool it. The first experiment took place on 6 February, two weeks after the eruption started. Påll holds a proud finger to the air when he remembers the date. He logged his activity in a diary and has a fine memory for the detail. The islanders parked a fire engine on the edge of the harbour and directed the hose up the slope. They felt it was making a difference, although geologists may dismiss this as nonsense. Either way, the flow eased. The lava stopped. The entrance to the harbour narrowed but remained open.

The eruption ended on 3 July, but the mess remained and 400 of 1,345 houses in the town had disappeared forever. Photos taken that summer show rooftops emerging like icebergs from a sea of black. The first six months of 1973 left Heimaey with a post-apocalyptic hue. But at least there was a reason to come back.

'That summer, we cleared the town of 1.5 million cubic metres of ash,' Påll recalls. Most of it laid the foundations for a new housing development on the southern edge of the town. The rest bulked up the runway at the airfield, which had previously been too narrow to meet regulations. Geothermic energy from the eruption heated the water supply on the island for years.

I ask Påll about the human casualty, the one member of the rescue team who died during the eruption. Påll walks back along the corridor and points out of the window beyond the photocopier.

'That house there, the third house from here with the rusty blue roof. It was in February. He went in through a window on the second floor because the ash was so high in the area around. He went down to the basement. It was full of gas and he died immediately.'

I leave Påll's office and turn right towards Eldfell. The street ends abruptly at a wall of black rock. Basalt dissects suburbia. A narrow footpath takes over from the tarmac. It leads up on to the lava field, decorated with outbreaks of purple flowers.

Every few steps a plaque displays the name of the house entombed 15m below. The houses probably look much the same today as in 1973. The rock will have infiltrated every corner of every room, but it will have prevented damp and decay. The plates will be in the kitchen cupboard. The cutlery will still be in the drawer. The children's toys will be in the same box. The clock will still stand on the mantelpiece, right twice a day.

There are ten minutes until kick-off when Björg bundles into the living room with a can of Pilsner and a glass. Like everyone else on the island, she has rushed home from work for the start of the match.

'There were a couple of people in the liquor store,' she pants, 'but everyone else is already at home.'

For the third time in a fortnight, the country is easing to a 90-minute halt. Iceland face Croatia in the final group match. Argentina and Nigeria play at the same time. Iceland must beat Croatia to progress to the knockout stage. Iceland also need Argentina to beat Nigeria, but not too emphatically and not by a greater margin than Iceland beat Croatia.

Björg draws the curtains while running through the permutations, and the mountain that shields the harbour disappears from view. There is a picture of a puffin in every room of the house. The one in this room is particularly pleased with itself, having posed for the photographer with a clump of sand eels in its bill.

Two more spectators crash through the door as the rhythmic thud of 'Seven Nation Army' marks the arrival of the teams on the pitch. Elfur, Björg's 17-year-old son, wriggles into the central spot on the sofa, a can of Coke in hand. His friend Hulda nestles under a blanket on the armchair. She is ambivalent to football – usually. Her boyfriend is half-Croatian and his support for the opposition has strengthened her sense of loyalty to Iceland, but not to the extent that it overcomes her pessimism. She predicts a 5-0 defeat.

Croatia have made nine changes from their mauling of Argentina, yet they dominate the early stages with arrowed passes and cushioned touches. They are in Iceland's category of high-achieving small nations. Just four million people live in Croatia but their team has a spine of gnarled, technical players who set the rhythm for the biggest clubs in the world.

The match is ten minutes old when one such player, Luka Modrić of Real Madrid, glides to the edge of Iceland's box. He contorts his body, ready to shoot. The screen freezes. We look at each other while Elfur fiddles with the settings. The screen stays frozen. Modrić, blurred around the edges, watches the ball with perfect clarity, an omnipotent puppet master suspended in time by patchy connectivity.

After ten long seconds, Björg snaps. 'I'm calling Vodafone.'

I reach to the armrest for my phone and scroll through Twitter while the call connects. I feel a flicker of adrenaline. Lionel Messi has scored. Argentina lead Nigeria. One goal is enough for Iceland.

Elfur stabs at the remote, Hulda texts, Björg speaks frantically to the customer service rep working the least desirable shift in Iceland. She cups her hand over the phone to provide an update.

'They're fixing it,' she whispers. 'Until the picture comes back, the lady on the phone is going to commentate for us.'

Björg returns the phone to her ear. Her brow furrows. She listens intently. The other three of us wait, the final link in this unorthodox communication chain.

'Nothing much happening,' she reports. 'Birkir Bjarnason has been elbowed in the face. He's bleeding everywhere. The doctors are with him. He's ruining a white towel ...'

The screen flickers and returns to Rostov, where Birkir plugs his left nostril with a tube of tissue. One goal. Iceland need one goal.

I am leaning forwards now, more hopeful. Iceland have the momentum. They are playing to their strengths and chiselling away at the Croatian defence. Alfreð Finnbogason misses a chance, unable to build on his goal in the first match. When Croatia fleetingly regain possession, the Icelanders chase like terriers hunting a wounded rabbit. It is a matter of *when* rather than *if* Iceland will score. Birkir, with his newly hooked nose that can smell around corners, squanders the next chance. Half-time creeps closer. Aron Gunnarsson tries to land the next blow, curling a shot towards the top corner that draws a flailing save from the Croatian keeper. The referee blows his whistle and the interval arrives at the worst possible time.

Hulda uses the half-time break to monitor Rúrik Gíslason's progress on Instagram. The lavishly handsome winger came on as a substitute for 30 minutes against Argentina and his Instagram account detonated. He had 30,000 followers at the start of the match. Half an hour of disciplined wing play boosted that number to almost 400,000. Most of his new admirers were young South American women. One photo of Rúrik caught their collective gaze, in which he is bronzed, topless and standing up to his waist in a serene lake.

'He's up to a million now,' Hulda reveals before glancing up at the screen to nonchalantly reveal that she is related to one of the pundits.

The second half starts and Croatia are roused. Milan Badelj wallops a shot against the crossbar after a few minutes. Shortly after, the same player hits the target with a volley that thuds into the ground and loops beyond Hannes Halldórsson and in. Elfur breaks the silence.

'Fuck,' he spits with staccato ferocity.

Almost simultaneously the commentator reveals in a rueful tone that Nigeria have equalised in the other match. The permutations lurch away from Iceland. The flurry of missed chances in the first half becomes increasingly painful with each passing minute.

Twenty minutes of attrition follow. And then, a lifeline. Dejan Lovren jerks his left arm and glances the ball inside the box. The referee purses his lips around the whistle and points to the spot. Penalty.

'I feel sorry for the referee,' Hulda muses as the Croatian players remonstrate and draw imaginary squares to call for the additional eyes of the video referee. 'He has to run around for the whole game but has no chance of winning,' she says. It is one of those comments – at once obvious and profound – that can only come from someone with a healthy detachment from the sport, someone unburdened by hackneyed cliché and the acknowledged templates for observation.

Gylfi interrupts my thoughts. With ice-cold blood coursing through his veins, he lifts the ball into the roof of the net. We celebrate with reserved fist pumps, but a happy ending seems distant as full time approaches. Five minutes remain. Then, from the other side of Russia, there is news. Marcos Rojo has scored for Argentina. The equation is simple. If Iceland score, they are through to the knockout stages of the World Cup.

'Now I actually care a bit,' Hulda announces, shuffling forwards in her chair. The dream flickers back to life.

I imagine how a goal would feel. I imagine the senseless ecstasy. I imagine how Vestmannaeyjar would react to the blackout joy. I think about Biggi and his crew and if there would be enough space on the trawler to contain their celebrating limbs. There are certain moments when we focus on one thing with such ferocity that everything else becomes numb. The last scene of a film, the final page of a book, the last round of a boxing bout when both fighters are slugging it out in a sepia haze of sweat and water. This is one of those moments. One goal.

Ivan Perišić delivers reality with a clinical thud of his left foot. Emil Hallfreðsson concedes possession cheaply and the sinewy winger punishes him with the goal that seals Iceland's fate.

We sit in silence as the players stumble around the pitch in numb devastation. Their eyes are dead with fatigue. Like the bystanders who gawp at the scene of a car accident, it is difficult to look away. The dejection is distilled because Argentina complied with their side of the bargain by beating Nigeria but not by too much. Iceland's fate was in their own hands, but it slipped away.

One by one, the Icelanders face the camera. Heimir rues that his team played five good halves of football at the tournament but let themselves down in the second period against Nigeria. Gylfi draws motivation from the defeat. He says in his soft, high-pitched voice that Iceland will just go to the Euros in 2020. They will go again. Aron Gunnarsson talks of pride and the honour of leaving everything on the pitch.

Jóhann Berg Guðmundsson delivers the most striking interview. His face is ashen. Beads of sweat glisten on his cheekbones, imitating the tears that he holds back.

'We didn't come here to make up the numbers,' he mumbles, his voice on the brink. 'We wanted to get through.'

The romance of the Icelandic story is seductive. Iceland are assigned the role of plucky underdogs with the dentist manager and the goalkeeper who directed a Eurovision music video. Heimir and the players acknowledge the seduction of this portrayal, but it does grate. Iceland do not excel because of Viking claps or bearded supporters in horned helmets. They excel because they are a good team. They are well organised, cohesive, tactically mature and smattered with star players.

With misty eyes, Jóhann Berg delivered a clear reminder of what is so impressive about Iceland. They were not in Russia for a selfie in Red Square. They were there to win matches, and what is more, they had a team capable of doing so. There comes a point when the romanticisation of the story obfuscates that achievement.

# Afterword

MANY PEOPLE have asked the same question: what does the future hold for Icelandic football? Some say Iceland will return to obscurity in a puff of acrid smoke, gone as quickly as they arrived. Indeed, Iceland's first match after the 2018 World Cup was a 6-0 defeat to Switzerland. As a 4-4 draw against the Swiss in 2013 was formative for this generation of Icelandic players, there was a sense of the circle being completed. Iceland had passed Switzerland on the way up. Now they were passing them on the way down. Yet a little over a month later, Iceland secured a creditable 2-2 draw against France, the world champions.

I would be bluffing if I were to chart Iceland's path with any certainty. Knowledge of the past does not signify an ability to read the future. That said, I shall offer a tentative prediction: Iceland will regress to the mean. They will reach a plateau of quality that is higher than what came before 2010, but lower that the sweet-spot years from 2014 to 2018. Iceland will continue to produce excellent players but will struggle to produce a team as good as the one we have seen in this period. There are two reasons for this.

First, Iceland now produces players with exceptional technical ability. Tight spaces and acute angles are no obstacle for the modern Icelandic player. This is a product of pristine facilities and skilled coaches. It is also what the export market demands. English, Dutch and German academies want players with confidence, technique and a brain that maps the spaces on a pitch. The style Iceland use, however, demands different qualities – positional discipline, energy and tactical rigidity. A conflict may arise between the type of player Iceland produces and the type of player Iceland needs to play defensive, low-possession football.

Second, the 'golden generation' of players born between 1988 and 1990 all emerged at a similar time. They settled into a national team that played without pressure or expectation, which allowed them to forge cohesive relationships at a gentle pace. Their replacements will not have the same luxury.

As a broader observation, it is no coincidence that Icelandic success has coincided with equilibrium between amateurism and professionalism. Viðar Halldórsson – professor of sociology at the University of Iceland – argues that Iceland has become more professional, but not too professional.

While the vast majority of players in Iceland supplement their football income with work or study, the sport has certainly professionalised. The players behave like elite athletes, they have access to good facilities and the expertise of well-educated coaches from Iceland and abroad. Nutrition, analysis and training methods are not far behind professional standards in Denmark or Norway.

Yet, on the other hand, Icelandic football still maintains an amateur spirit whereby the purpose of sport is enjoyment, which creates an environment that prioritises camaraderie and creativity. Football clubs in Iceland exist for, and because of, the local community. Children can cycle to their local club and know that the doors will be open, from when they are aged four until they are 19, regardless of their ability. Participation is more important than performance.

The longer Icelandic football can surf this state of equilibrium, the longer the national team will compete with the elite.

There is a precedent for Nordic national teams drastically improving shortly after the advent of professionalism. The amateur era ended in Denmark in 1978; eight years later, the 'Danish Dynamite' team made a strong impression at the 1986 World Cup before becoming European champions in 1992.

Similarly, once football in Norway became professional in 1991 the national team qualified for the 1994 World Cup – its first in 56 years – and reached the last 16 at the 1998 World Cup.

The trajectories of Denmark and Norway in the 21st century must serve as a warning: both regressed as the strive for professionalism and commercialism eroded amateur values.

As a final thought, Iceland occupies a unique space between Europe and the USA. Geographical isolation will prevent Iceland integrating with the European knowledge network to the same extent as Spain, for example. But there is significant value in looking the other way across the Atlantic.

The presence of an American airbase on Iceland from the Second World War until 2006 was divisive, but it did symbolise a form of mid-Atlanticism that endures today. In the last decade Iceland has positioned itself as a stopover destination for transatlantic flights. The departures board at Keflavík airport reads as a list of American east-coast cities, with Los Angeles and San Francisco thrown in for balance. It is not uncommon to hear the gurgle of squat American pickup trucks in Reykjavík, while the proliferation of various craft beer establishments in the capital has a distinct stateside tinge.

This mid-Atlantic identity has also crept into football. Brynjar Benediktsson and Jóna Kristín Hauksdóttir are the co-founders of Soccer and Education USA, an agency that helps talented Icelandic footballers obtain scholarships to study at American colleges or universities. Brynjar and Jóna both represented Iceland at youth level before moving to Clemson University in South Carolina to study economics. They present college soccer as a viable alternative to the traditional routes to professional football that pass through the Scandinavian leagues or academies in the Netherlands and England.

It is an easier sell to women, given the high standard of women's soccer in the United States compared to most of Europe. But it also appeals to Icelandic parents who value the importance of formal education, and almost every Icelandic parent falls in that category. A dream of making it in Spain or England can fade but a degree certificate is forever.

The United States is a hotbed of sporting innovation. European football coaches are increasingly influenced by ideas emerging from the big four American sports: basketball, American football, baseball and ice hockey. The proximity of soccer to these innovations means that, as the sport develops and extends its reach with the United States, it will form a fertile knowledge network of its own.

The links that Brynjar and Jóna are forging (they have secured scholarships for more than 60 Icelandic footballers since 2016), coupled with the reimagination of Keflavík airport as a transport hub linking Europe to the United States, means Iceland is uniquely positioned to straddle two networks. It can draw the best from both.

When the Albania national team visited Iceland in 1990, the match descended into a farce of duty-free theft and nude pitch invasions. As Einar Már Guðmundsson sagely observed: 'Reality is always catching realism by surprise.' That is what makes this story so enchanting. Nobody, not even the most sanguine of Icelanders, predicted the emergence of such a successful team. Of course, we can look back with hindsight and identify the decisions, traits, socio-cultural conditions and downright good fortune that made it possible. But this outsider surprised everyone when it found a way into the inner circle.

The successful outsider, the underdog, brings elite sport closer to those of us who will never experience its thrill for ourselves. The outsider becomes one of us. The Iceland team of boys next door, many of whom grew up together, make football feel tangible, relatable, when so many aspects of the game appear to be increasingly detached from reality.

The Icelandic story reins football in from the clouds and back to the ground.